Gentlemen in Red

Gentlemen in Red

Two Accounts of
British Infantry Officers
During the Peninsular War

Recollections of an
Old 52nd Man

by John Dobbs

An Officer of Fusiliers

by Robert Knowles

LEONAUR

*Gentlemen in Red: Two Accounts of British Infantry Officers
During the Peninsular War
Recollections of an Old 52nd Man* by John Dobbs
An Officer of Fusiliers by Robert Knowles

Published by Leonaur Ltd

Text in this form and material original to this edition
copyright © 2008 Leonaur Ltd

ISBN: 978-1-84677-480-5 (hardcover)
ISBN: 978-1-84677-479-9 (softcover)

http://www.leonaur.com

Contents

Recollections of an Old 52nd Man   7

An Officer of Fusiliers   105

Recollections of an Old 52nd Man

John Dobbs

Contents

Introduction   11

First Days of Campaigning   19

The Peninsula Again   36

Storming Badajoz   55

St Sebastian   69

Into France   76

Home Again   93

Introduction

My father, Francis Dobbs, Esq., barrister-at-law, and member of Parliament, was descended from an officer of rank in Queen Elizabeth's army, who settled in the North of Ireland, and married a granddaughter of O'Neill, Earl of Tyrone. My father was rather remarkable as a public character. He took an active part in the politics of his day, as a writer, and as a speaker in the House of Commons; also, in the Irish Volunteers, being reviewing Major to Lord Charlemont. He neglected his profession for these public matters to the injury of his private affairs. My mother, daughter of Alexander Stuart, of Ballintoy, a branch of the Bute family, was left a widow, with very limited means, when I was ten years old. We then resided in Dublin.

The first public event which made an impression on me was the Irish rebellion of 1798. I was then seven years old. Four hundred thousand united Irishmen were banded together for the overthrow of the British Government in Ireland, and had promises of assistance from the French Government, who had attempted to land fifteen thousand men at Bantry Bay in 1796, but were prevented by a violent storm. In 1798 the rebellion broke out, and the French sent another fleet, with three thousand five hundred men, who were to land in the North of Ireland. This fleet was defeated by Sir John B. Warren; most of the ships were taken. Another fleet succeeded in landing nine hundred men at Kilala; they advanced into the interior, and were defeated at Ballynamuck by our troops. At this time the defence of Ireland depended on her Militia (and some of the Southern regiments were not to be depended on, having a number of sworn rebels in them) and corps of Yeomanry, which were formed wherever a sufficient body of loyal subjects could be collected. Their number was 82,941, of which 11,000 were cavalry—they were principally from the Northern counties. In Dublin there were the Lawyers, Attorneys, Merchants, and College Corps, and several others, amongst which, one called Beresford's, bore a prominent part. The loyal male members of every family were attached to one of them; and on the ringing of the alarm bells, and the drums beating to arms, each repaired to the alarm post of his corps, leaving the women and children in a state of anxiety.

My father, four brothers, uncle, and four first cousins, were at this time under arms for the defence of Ireland. My brother William commanded a company of the Armagh Militia at Ballynamuck, and my brother Francis was engaged with the Lisburn Yeomanry at Ballynahinch.

On the 1st August, 1798, Nelson attacked the French fleet, consisting of 13 sail of the line, and some smaller vessels, with twelve British ships of the line in the Nile, and after a bloody engagement took: nine of them, and burnt two more. He also captured two frigates, and a number of gun boats. In Dublin the rejoicings for this victory were most enthusiastic; every house was illuminated from top to bottom. It was a grand sight. Splendid transparencies were to be seen in every direction, and the streets were crowded by all classes, in their best attire.

In 1806 Nelson's destruction of the combined fleets of France and Spain, off Trafalgar, put an end to Bonaparte's hopes of invading England, his fleets being all but annihilated. He had prepared, at Boulgne, for the above purpose, a camp of one hundred and sixty thousand men, and an immense flotilla of flat-bottomed boats and gun-boats. These boats were to have been rowed across during the first heavy fog. At this time Bonaparte's allies included all the continental powers with the exception of Sweden.

In the same year, I being fifteen years old, Lord Gosford gave me a Lieutenancy in the Armagh Militia, in which my brother Francis was Captain, I joined them at Ennis, in the County Clare, whence we marched to Tuam, in Galway, when I had some hard night duty, *still hunting*. We had a subaltern's guard here, and the guard-room was infested with rats. While sleeping on the guard bed, I was awakened by a troop of them making off with the candle which was lighting on the table.

We were then sent to Eyrcourt, leaving detachments at Banagher and Shannon Bridge, at which places I was successively stationed. While here, our men were trained to the great guns in the batteries. During my stay at Shannon Bridge, my brother and I visited Ballinasloe during the great fair held there, and were witnesses to a great faction fight. There was a large body on each side, and they fought with sticks and stones to the terror of all persons peaceably inclined. All the shops were closed, shutters put up, and business suspended. Such was the state of most of the large towns in Ireland, and it continued so till after Peel's Act for the establishment of the present police. Soon afterwards we were removed to Naas, near Dublin, where I received my appointment to the 52nd (Sir John Moore being an old schoolfellow of my fathers), in which regiment my brother Joseph was a captain. Having gone out in the expedition to Ferrol as a volunteer, he distinguished himself in boarding a Spanish vessel, in consequence of which he received his commission in the 52nd. His services in the 52nd will be mentioned in my recollections of that corps. My brother Alexander entered the Navy, and after many boat services he particularly distinguished himself on the lakes of Canada. In the capture of Oswago, and Fort Erie, on which lake we had not an armed vessel, while the Americans had three armed schooners with a crew of 35 men each, being 105 men, and 92 lbs of metal. They were anchored off the fort, a short distance above the falls of Niagara in a position calculated to prevent its attack by our troops.

My brother, who was in command of the *Charwell* and *Nancy* below the falls of Niagara, took 75 of his men and gig, which they landed below the fall, at Queenstown, carrying it for twenty miles on their shoulders, and launched it into Lake Erie, at Frenchman's Creek,where he procured five *batteaux* with which he succeeded in boarding and carrying two of the schooners. The third, by cutting her cable, got away, leaving the boats struggling with the rapids above the fall, from which they had a narrow escape. He then assisted the troops in the capture of the fort. Afterwards receiving a wound in the head,—the effects of which hastened his death. For his services at Fort Erie he was made C.B., and posted, he being only a commander in command of the fleet on Lake Erie. My brother William had a company in the Armagh Militia, and distinguished himself during the rebellion in the action in Ballynamuck. He died from fever, contracted while on guard at Kilmainham. My brother Francis volunteered from the Armagh Militia with one hundred men just before the peace, and got a company in the 12th Foot, but was reduced to half pay before the period, when it would have become permanent. The 52nd regiment was employed in North America from 1765 to 1778, taking a distinguished part in the battle of Bunker's Hill, and the various operations with the United States; in India from 1783 to 1793, taking a distinguished part in the operations which led to the conquest of the Misore and the island of Ceylon.

In 1799 they got a second battalion, and 1800 both battalions were employed in the expedition to Ferrol, in which they took an active part in what little was done; in 1803 the 2nd battalion was made the 96th Regiment, and the 1st battalion made light infantry, being the picked men of both battalions. In 1804 a 2nd battalion was again added from 1803 to 1808; the 1st battalion was employed in Sicily.

In 1807 the 2nd battalion was employed in taking Copenhagen, and the Danish fleet which Buonaparte was about employing against us.

The 1st battalion embarked for Sweden on the 30th of April 1808, and arrived at Gottenburg on the 17th May, from whence it sailed for England on the 3rd of July, and arrived at Spithead on the 21st August. The 2nd battalion had preceded the 1st embarking on the 16th July, and landing in Portugal on the 19th of August, took an active part, in the Battle of Vimiera on the 21st.

The 1st battalion sailed from Corunna on the 17th January, 1809, and arrived in England on the 25th.

The 2nd battalion sailed from Viga on the 13th January, and landed at Ramsgate the end of the month.

The 1st battalion again embarked for Portugal on the 25th of May, 1809, and landed at Lisbon on the 5th of July, and joined Lord Wellington's army at Talavera after a forced march of sixty-two miles in twenty-six hours, and served in the Peninsula up to the end of the war.

The origin of the 52nd regiment, dated from the eve of the commencement of the contest known in history as the Seven Years' War, the French having raised a powerful navy, the peace of Aix-la-Chapelle was soon broken, and in the winter of 1755 the attack made by them in the British settlement beyond the Alleghany Mountains in North America hastened the crisis, when, therefore, war between the two countries was inevitable; an augmentation was made to the army, and in December, 1755, eleven regiments of infantry were raised, which have since been retained, and numbered from the 50th to the 60th inclusive, becoming part of the celebrated Light Division covering the retreat to the lines, and taking a prominent part in the battle of Busaco, defence of the lines of Torres Vedras, advance after Massenas retreating army, combat of Sabugal, battle of Fuentes d'Onor, sieges of Rodrigo and Badajos, battle of Salamanca, taking of Madrid and covering the Burgas retreat, advance and taking of Burgos affair at St. Milan and battle of Vittoria, battles of the Pyrenees, storming the heights of Vera, battles of Nivelle, Nive, Orthes and Toulouse in 1814.

In 1816, although the regiment did not get credit for it in the Duke's dispatch after the battle of Waterloo, it is now ascertained, without contradiction, that the defeat of the young guard was by the 52nd Regiment under Lord Seaton, and the total route of the French army the result. It bears on its colours:

Hindostan	Vittoria
Vimiera	Nivelle
Corunna	Nive
Busaco	Orthes
Fuentes d'Onor	Toulouse
Ciudad Rodrigo	Peninsula
Badajos	Waterloo
Salamanca	

A regiment never surpassed in arms since arms
were first borne by men.
W. Napier, Nivelle, 1813

The junior veterans of the Peninsular War have to thank a 52nd man for their services being recognised by Her Majesty. While the Duke of Wellington opposed the medal, and all the inferior officers who had themselves been decorated, backed him or hung back. The Duke of Richmond stood out and maintained their cause and the medal was granted on the 1st of June, 1847, after many of them had ceased to exist, and thirty-three years after it terminated, at which time I received a medal and ten clasps for Corunna, Fuentes d'Onor, Ciudad Rodrigo, Badajos, Salamanca, Vittoria, Pyrenees, St. Sabastian, Nivelle, and Nive.

While we, the left wing under Sir John Hope, protected the flank of the main army from 15,000 picked troops behind the walls of Bayonne, they got clasps for Orthes and Toulouse, while we got none, although engaged for fifty days and nights, which ended in a sortie, in which we lost Sir John Hope (taken prisoner), Gen. Hay killed and Sir Thomas Bradford wounded before it was driven back to its ramparts, and I was severely wounded by the last shot fired, and I believe the last shot fired in that war.

CHAPTER 1

First Days of Campaigning

On joining the 52nd Regiment, in 1808, I found myself in the midst of perfect gentlemen. The duty was carried on like clock work, and scarcely any wine drank at the mess, frequently none. After dinner we used to spend the evening playing foot-ball, rackets, &c.; we had constant roll-calls for eye washing; every man was paraded with the lid of his camp-kettle full of water which they washed them with. I was not allowed to take command of a section going to church till I finished my drill. In drill every man was taught his centre of gravity by the balance step,—to take an exact length of pace by the pace stick,—to step in slow, quick and double quick, by the plummet and tap of the drum, afterwards to move in bodies or extended order and out post duty, &c.

The officers having to go through every part of it, the drill was brought to such perfection that a line of 1000 men has been known to march over Shorncliff without any perceptible departure from their dressing.

Shortly after I had been dismissed from drill the regiment joined Sir John Moore's expedition to Sweden, and I take this opportunity to mention some of the disadvantages we then laboured under. We had no marching money, no prince's allowance or sea-stock provided, and had to lay in our own. We were obliged to prepare for a much longer period than the voyage was likely to last, from the uncertainty of sailing vessels; a voyage which could now be performed in a day, at that time frequently occupied weeks.

The vessel I embarked in was an old merchantman, of about two hundred tons, called the *Three Brothers*, Reynett and Dobbs companies, two hundred strong, with seven officers, were its occupants. The cabin had two births on each side, one over the other—these were of course chosen by the four seniors, while the three juniors slept in cots swung to the ceiling, and only a few inches apart. They were afterwards increased to nine, the two added placed the two juniors on the floor, one on each side of the table which was in the centre. The first thing to be done by our servants was to remove the five moveable beds, and after we had washed to arrange the cabin for breakfast the table was lashed to the floor. In a gale of wind one day, the lashing gave way while we were at dinner, and threw Captain Reynett (now Lieut.-General Sir John) against the bulkhead, emptying a tureen of pea-soup on his head, which was the cause of some amusement to those who escaped the disaster, and our caterer, (now Sir T. E. Drake) also gave us a laugh by the way he recommended the ration pork, pressing each number of the mess to partake of it, till at last some of us observed that he never eats any himself, and he was asked why, in answer to which, he said, my good fellows, my mother told me never to make a beast of myself. The plan in the 52nd was to laugh each other out of any eccentricities we observed, and accordingly we attacked Maitland about his going over each dish commenting on the manner it was cooked, and they certainly would not bear comparison with what he sat down to, at Lord Londerdale's, his father. We remained in the *Three Brothers* during our stay in Sweden, and until our arrival on the coast of Portugal, where we landed the day after the battle of Vimiero. The vessel proceeded with our baggage to the Tagus, where she took in a shipful of French troops, sent home by the convention of Cintra. Shortly after leaving the Tagus, she foundered. Having encountered very rough weather in the Baltic Sea, English Channel, and Bay of Biscay, we had a fortunate escape.

On our way to Sweden we had to pass the Skagerrack in a dense fog, and against a head wind, while a large fleet were tacking, so that it was next to impossible to escape collision. We had drums beating, bugles blowing, bells ringing, and men shouting, having to avoid the enemy's shore on our right hand, and rocky islands on our left.

We arrived at Gottenburg on the 17th May, 1808, and returned to England in the beginning of July.

While lying in Gottenburg harbour, we were rather surprised to find the body of one of our men, who had been drowned bathing, after a length of time rising at the same spot. It appears there are no tides in the Baltic; another fact peculiar to that latitude also came under notice, *and that was daylight at the hour of midnight, at the time we were there.*

These men were frequently landed for exercise on an uninhabited island (of which there were many) in the harbour, and as it was full of hares, there was often a hunt after the first one seen, which was generally succeeded by several others being started, which caused a most exciting scene, the hunters separating into as many parties as there were hares.

We also had a boat's crew selected from our men, with which we could man one of the ships boats, and visit the other ships, or land on one of the islands for bathing, &c.

On one occasion my brother having dined on board one of the ships, I took the boat for him, it was blowing very fresh, and on our return came on to blow harder, so that we found it hard work to get back, and were nearly upset by getting foul of a ship's cable.

I visited Gottenburg, but cannot remember anything about it worthy of remark, except that the general appearance was pleasing. On leaving Gottenburg harbour, after a heavy gale of wind, we found ourselves in the midst of seven water-spouts. It was a grand sight; we passed through them without injury.

Having the morning watch while passing up the channel, from the Baltic, I was agreeably surprised by the smell of new-mown hay, We were not then in sight of the land, and it seemed particularly sweet from our having been so long on board. Having touched at Portsmouth we proceeded on our way to Portugal, touching at Plymouth, and were supplied with more flat-bottomed boats for landing men. We were subsequently obliged to put into Torbay from stress of weather, and it was some time before we could get out of the channel. After crossing the bay of Biscay, we got into a shoal of gurnets, it extended for a considerable distance, and could be seen at a considerable distance, and could be seen in its length and breadth, all the snouts of the fishes being above the surface, there was a number of herring hogs following and feeding on them, as the weather was calm, we were able to fish over the side catching them as fast as we could throw in our lines, we also caught some needle-fish, and at night the sea appeared to be on fire as we passed through it.

We landed near Vimiera on the 22nd August, 1808, in a heavy surf, with only the clothes we wore, one blanket and a few days' provisions in our haversacks, and bivouacked in the French huts that night. These huts were branches of trees with the butts on the ground, and the tops meeting, the small branches serving for thatch

Having arrived off the coast of Portugal on the 21st August, 1808, on which day our 2nd battalion took an active part in the battle of Vimiera, we got orders to land the following morning, and had to abandon any sea-stock, which we could not carry in our haversacks or canteens, and having a quantity of spruce beer, which was beginning to fly, our amusement the evening before was fixing a mark in the ceiling, and letting the corks fly at it. We attempted to land in the flat-bottomed boats, but, one or two of the first that attempted it were swamped by the surf, and the men drowned. It was therefore found necessary to use the men-at-war-boats, and we were changed into them, in which operation I had a narrow escape of losing my leg between the two boats; I however escaped with a severe bruise, which did not prevent me marching with the regiment. Immediately after landing on the 22nd, we had to cross over several extensive vineyards, to the great delight of the troops, who helped themselves to the grapes, the roots of which are at a short distance from one another, having been bared of the old branches for firing, the new branches are covered with clusters of them, the appearance at a little distance is like that of field peas, when ripe, they are carried into houses having a large shallow reservoir which they are spread over, having sufficient slope to let the juice run to a spout prepared for emptying it into casks ready for its reception. When the grapes are spread a number of persons, with not very clean feet, are sent into the reservoir, who tramp them till the juice runs off, after this, the skins are collected and put into the press, which is a coil of rope several feet high, a heavy beam moving on a pivot, being a powerful lever, presses the coil of rope till all the remaining juice is pressed out of them, the juice thus obtained, is allowed to ferment in large vessels. In Spain it is conveyed from place to place, in pigskins turned inside out, and coated with tar, they are slung on the backs of mules, whose pack saddles are well adapted for the service; when exposed to the heat of the sun, and the skins not very new, the tar and hair become blended with the wine which becomes anything but agreeable. Wine was frequently issued in place of the ration-rum, and until accustomed to it, it was considered a grand thing by the men, to be drinking wine.

To the great joy of the men, they were relieved from hair-tying which was a burden grievous to be borne. And our huts being close to those occupied by the men, we could hear them joking one another on the subject; one of the principal ones was calling on their comrade to tie them, which was impossible, as their hair was gone.

Our first days march was a short one, but the weight each man had to carry was tremendous in addition to heavy knapsacks; there were their muskets and accoutrements, seventy rounds of ammunition, a blanket, a mess kettle, and wooden canteen. They and their officers had three day's provisions. The weather was very hot; our caps and leather stocks gave us great annoyance—the former by day, and the latter, both day and night. As we slept in our clothes we remedied the former by boring two small holes in the sides, and the officers, the latter, by clasping them over the knee; the men, by slipping them over the ramrod. We, each of us, had a small tin tot which we carried with a knife and fork, made to shut up like a common clasp knife. The tot was in constant requisition. On getting up it was paraded with water to wash my mouth; at breakfast, it answered for a teacup, on the march, for drinking out of, at dinner, for soup, after dinner, for rum, punch, or wine. After some time I supplied its place with a small silver cup for the same uses; also, a silver fork, both of which, being easily cleaned, were great luxuries.

As we had no change of clothes till our arrival in Lisbon, we had to take advantage of some running stream, and wash our shirts as well as we could, sitting by till they dried. We were billeted in Lisbon for several days, and took the opportunity of visiting remarkable places about it, amongst others a gambling house greatly frequented, and were surprised to find the most active persons to be the priests and monks, some of them partners in the concern. As I passed through the streets, every corner had a woman frying and selling sardines, which appeared very plenty, and gave occupation to a great many fishermen, who had an image of their patron saint in the bow of each boat with a small begging-box under it, having a slit in the top, and lock attached. As their prayers are addressed to the saint for success in their fishing, when they are disappointed, they fly into a rage with the saint, and duck his image, giving him all sort of abuse. The key of the money box is kept by a priest, who relieves it of its contents from time to time.

Another thing which strikes a stranger is, the constant assassinations, a number of bodies being found every morning—some stabbed by enemies, others by bravos, hired for the purpose. What applies to Lisbon is equally applicable to all the larger towns and cities in Spain and Portugal. When billeted in Oporta, at the end of the war, the native merchant on whom I was billeted, told me the following anecdote which was told himself by a friend:

That, having in a fit of anger, hired a bravo to murder a friend, On becoming calm he went to the bravo's house to prevent his doing the deed. The man not being at home, he asked where he was to be found. The answer was, at church, to which he followed him, and observed him earnestly engaged in his devotions. As soon as they were over, he joined him, and after letting him know that he had changed his mind, and would not have the man murdered, he asked him how he could engage in prayer when about to commit such an act. The bravo replied that he was asking for success in the job.

The weapon used for assassinations is a stiletto. It has a straight-handle and blade, the latter tapering to a point. It is carried in the sleeve, and when about to use it, the handle is turned with the blade backwards along the arm, which hides it from observation. The bravo passes the person on the left side, giving him a back-stroke which strikes into the heart, he still moving on as if nothing had happened.

They are very dexterous in throwing it. This is done by laying the handle in the palm, with the blade outward, and with a jerk discharging it up, down, or straightforward, with so certain an aim as to strike a mark of one penny piece at twelve paces distance.

The building occupied by the inquisition was not to be

seen, but the inquisition itself had been suppressed by the French, not only in Lisbon, but throughout the Peninsula. In Madrid the whole system was exposed by them. All the subterranean apartments having been discovered by one of their engineers, who suspected them to be under the Chapel, he poured a quantity of water on the flags, which found its way through the joining on the flag that covered the stair cases leading to them.

It is a slur upon the English that the French have done more to suppress this dreadful institution, than the English authorities who call themselves Protestants.

The 52nd having crossed the Tagus, a little above Lisbon, marched through the Alentejo. Our first days march was distressing from want of water—not a drop being to be had from the time we started till we got into quarters for the night. The consequence was, that the men fell out by hundreds, but even this had some advantage, as they marked the road for those in the rear.

While on the advance to Estremoz, we met the French garrison of Elvas on its way to Lisbon for embarkation, as agreed on in the convention of Cintra. Having halted in this neighbourhood, an Irishman of the name of Patrick Donovan deserted to us. It appeared that he had been implicated in the Irish rebellion, and had been banished to the Continent. He said he had been made a present of to the King of Prussia, and entered his services. When that country had become subject to Buonaparte, he had been transferred to the French army, and shared in most of Buonaparte's victories. He had now made his escape with a hope of getting home to his country. He was a noble soldier; he joined my brother's company, and served through the Peninsula campaign. His experience of French tactics, and his fear of being recaptured kept him always on the alert, and when he found us careless, he would caution us to be on our guard, and always kept a sharp lookout himself.

We waited till the beginning of November at Estremoz, and enjoyed the fruits of that country in all their perfection, melons, water melons, oranges, figs, grapes, and what I observed at Lisbon, as it regards sardines, might be observed here and elsewhere of chestnuts, every corner having stoves for roasting them. We were greatly annoyed by the constant ringing of the church bells; they never ceased. We were also surprised to find a list of sins and prohibited articles of food hung at each church door, with a price attached, for which they might be indulged in, a bell was made a Christian, and got a name. We never paraded for Protestant worship, but were paraded for a Roman Catholic ceremony, and presented arms to the host as it passed, which did not give us any concern at that time. At this place I witnessed the interment of a beautiful young female in one of the churches. She was in full dress, and was carried on a bier. A flag had been taken up and a grave dug, in which she was laid, and when a few inches of clay had been laid over her, they began to pound it with a piece of wood, made like a paving *mallet,* until nearly all the earth taken out was forced back.

In the beginning of November, 1808, we entered Spain. In the first village we had a sample of Spanish welcome; we were told that we were not wanted, that they could fight their own battles without our help, &c.

A number of houses were told off for our company's quarters, but we had great difficulty in getting in, the doors being closed against us. One of the houses appeared to be untenanted, and we were going to break the door open, when an old woman put her head out of a window over it, and then held out an old matchlock gun, in order to frighten us away, her hand shaking with age and fright. When we got to Salamanca we found a change for the better, at least I did; the old lady on whom I was billeted used to send me a cup of chocolate, and a thin slice of toast every morning before I was up, and paid every attention to my comfort, while I remained with her, which was till the 11th of December, 1808.

On the 23rd we were cantoned at Schagun, after Lord Paget with his Hussars had driven the French Dragoons out of it. At this time Napoleon, with sixty thousand men, was marching from Madrid to intercept us, while Soult had thirty thousand in our front, and we were only twenty-two thousand. Sir John Moore's object was to give the Spaniard's an opportunity to rally, by drawing off the French force, but it was of no use.

On the 23rd of December, 1808, we had a night march to attack Soult. The snow lay on the ground several inches deep, and we were forbidden to speak. Unexpectedly, about midnight, the word was passed from the rear to counter-march, and we returned to our quarters. On the 25th we were in full retreat, the reserve in which the 52nd were being the rear-guard, with the exception of the Hussar Brigade, who remained behind till we entered the mountains, and then passed us.

At Benevente, Buonaparte overtook, but failed in intercepting us, when he made his appearance on the heights over the bridge, the Reserve got under arms, and drew up in front of the town, the Hussar Brigade being on the plain, between us and the river, with their picquets at the bridges and forts. On this occasion, for the first and last time, I saw Napoleon I; he had a numerous staff in attendance; but, my brother's glass being a good one, I was able to distinguish him, as he reconnoitered us. Finding that we had slipped through his fingers, he took his departure after seeing his Imperial Guard very roughly handled by the Hussar Brigade, who were left behind while we continued our retreat. On this occasion the French lost a general and seventy prisoners, with a number of men killed and wounded.

Just before the enemy's advance to Cacabelas, the Reserve were halted on the heights above it for the purpose of hanging three marauders. Everything was ready, and a square formed round the gallows, when a hussar rode in from the rear, reporting to General Paget that the enemy was close at hand. He coolly received the report, and proceeded to address the troops, stating the disgrace attached to the crime, but that he would pardon them if they would refrain from such excess; but that, if this promise was not made, they should die, if the enemy were firing into the square. There was a general exclamation of "We will! we will!" He made a sign to the Provost Marshal, who immediately liberated the prisoners. The troops were at once moved off—some to cover the retreat on this side of the river, while others crossed and took up a position to cover their retreat over the bridges. After repulsing the enemy, the retreat was continued. It may be well to state that Sir John Moore superintended the various operations necessary to retard the advancing enemy, taking advantage of every height and defile, placing a gun where it could tell on their advance, and throwing a shrapnel shell, so as to discharge itself into a column of infantry or cavalry, as required., This was our occupation by day, which delay had to be made up for at night. The want of rest made us subject to optical illusions—one remarkable one I think worthy of mention. The head of the column came to a small stream running across the road (which became magnified in their sight) to a broad river of unknown depth. The front rank halted, and, of course, all in their rear did the same, and all sat down in mud nearly knee deep, and at once fell fast asleep. Some staff officer discovered the mistake, or it is likely we should have remained till morning.

There was a great deal of suffering from dysentery, and there were prisoners taken by the enemy in consequence of men being obliged to fall out. In this the Highlanders had a great advantage over the Reserve, who wore trousers.

As there is a prejudice against low-sized men, the fact that the lowest man in my brother's company (I don't think he was five feet three inches, men being scarce in those days) in addition to his own knapsack, carried that of our right hand man for the latter part of the retreat, who was fully six feet high, breadth making up for length. The retreat of the reserve occupied 18 days, the distance was about 230 miles. The French army under Soult, after Napoleon had left him, was sixty thousand men and ninety guns, while Sir John Moore's army only consisted of nineteen thousand, three thousand having been sent to Vigo. During the greater part of this retreat, we had to march all night and halt by day, to allow the baggage, stores, and stragglers to get off; when we moved on, the rear files of the rifle corps, and the advance files of the enemy were constantly engaged. No new hand could stand the night work; some officers who joined us on the retreat, having come out with Sir David Baird to Corunna, were so ill after the first night's exposure that they had to go back to Corunna. The roads were nearly knee deep with mud, and part of the mountain with snow. When we got to Lugo, we were relieved for the night, and occupied a convent. All the officers of the 52nd were crowded into one small room, having closed the window-shutters and door, and having a charcoal pan lighting, our adjutant, who was the first to lie down, was seized with convulsions, but being carried out immediately recovered, which, showed us the danger we had escaped, and its cause.

Having offered battle to the enemy at Lugo, our baggage was sent to the rear, and unfortunately our rations, cloaks, and blankets were on the mules, and we never saw them again. One of the men having thrown away half his blanket to lighten himself, I picked it up, and turning down a foot of the end over a string, which I tied round my neck, it answered all the purposes of a cloak. Having got a bullock's heart from one of the butchers, we had it hot and cold for breakfast, dinner, and supper, till our rations became due. It may be imagined what we suffered during the rest of our retreat, again being the rear guard. Our shoes being worn out, we got some of those sent out, I believe for Spanish troops, and these being supplied by contract, were so bad that a few hours' marching left them without soles. In this state we arrived at Corunna, and were allowed to go into some houses in the neighbourhood.

During the retreat, we were in such need of rest that we often fell asleep whilst marching, and as I had to carry one of the colours, the unfortunate man in my front often suffered from the pole, whilst I, in return, frequently knocked my head against the butt end of his musket. None but staff officers were allowed to have horses. On our coming in sight of Corunna no fleet was there to convey us off, but it arrived shortly afterwards.

These divisions occupied the town and suburbs, the reserve was posted with its left at the village of El Buno and its right on the road to St. Iago Compostello. For twelve days these hardy soldiers had covered the retreat, during which time they had traversed eighty miles of road in two marches, passed several nights under arms in the snow at the mountains, were seven times engaged with the enemy, and they now assembled at the outposts having fewer men missing from the ranks (including those who had fallen in battle) than any other division in the army. An admirable instance of the value of good discipline, and a manifest proof of the malignant injustice with which Sir J. Moore has been accused of precipitating his retreat beyond the measure of human strength. On the morning of the 16th January, 1809, the day of the battle of Corunna, while preparing our breakfast of flour and milk, a tremendous explosion took place, and a quantity of matter from the roof fell into the vessels, completely spoiling the contents. This was caused by the destruction of the powder magazine which was done to prevent it falling into the hands of the enemy. On inspecting the quarters, the men lay as if dead over the floors, but the enemy had hardly fired his first gun before every man was up and ready for action, in which they immediately engaged.[1]

---

1. *Corunna and Napier,* vol. 1, page 488.

The late arrival of the transports, the increasing force of the enemy, and the disadvantageous nature of the ground augmented the difficulty and danger of the embarkation so much that several general officers proposed to the Commander-in-chief that he should negotiate for leave to retire to his ships unmolested. There was little chance of such a proposal being agreed to by the enemy, and there was no reason to try. The army had suffered but not from defeat, its situation was dangerous, but far from desperate, and the General would not consent to remove the standard of energy and prudence which marked his retreat by a negotiation that would have given an appearance of timidity and indecision to his previous operations as opposite to their real character as light is to darkness. His high spirit and clear judgement revolted at the idea, and he rejected the degrading advice without hesitation.

All the encumbrances of the army were shipped in the night of the 15th, and on the morning of the 16th, everything was prepared to withdraw the fighting men as soon as darkness would permit them to move without being perceived.[2]

The British had only 14,500 infantry in position at Corunna; they had no cavalry, the men being embarked and most of the horses shot; any fit for service were embarked with 52 pieces of artillery; and eight British 6-pounders and four Spanish guns were in position at the battle. The latter were not effective, our balls not fitting.

Their position was a high range which encircled a lower one occupied by our army. Their cavalry were on the left of the French eleven-gun battery, which commenced the action.

BATTLE OF CORUNNA

The village we occupied was about half a mile in the rear of General Hope's division. About three o'clock they opened

2. *Napier*, Vol 1, pages 492 and 3.

fire from a battery of eleven guns, which had been masked with straw. Under the cover of this fire he advanced to the attack in four columns, two of which attacked the right and centre; that on the right was met by the rifle corps, while that on the centre was received by Lord William Bentick; Brigadier-General Paget was ordered up with the reserve in support, and the 52nd ordered to relieve the Rifle Corps (their ammunition being expended and most of their swords out of order) which we did in extended order sending the colours to the rear. Sir Sidney Beckwith met us, calling out, "Come here with your bayonets, come here with your bayonets." Reynett's company, in which I was one of the first engaged, and the first man hit was close by me; he fell apparently dead by the ball, it having entered the forehead and passed out at the back of the head, so that I said nothing could be done for him; but what was my surprise afterwards to find he was not killed, the ball having passed round the head under the skin. On recovering his senses he was taken by some passers-by to the rear and re-embarked; he was recovering of the wound when he was attacked by fever and carried off. We continued to drive the enemy before us till getting on its left flank they had to withdraw the other column, attacking our centre at the village of Elvina, and return to the strong position which they had left for the attack.

DEATH OF SIR JOHN MOORE

Sir John Moore, while earnestly watching the result of the fight about the village of Elvina, was struck on the left breast by a canon shot; it threw him from his horse with violence; he rose again in a sitting posture, his countenance changed, and his steadfast eye still fixed upon the regiments engaged in his front. No sigh betrayed a sensation of pain, but in a few moments when he was satisfied that the troops were gaining ground, his countenance brightened and he suffered himself to be taken to the rear. Then was seen the dreadful nature of his hurt. The shoulders were shattered to pieces, the arm was hanging by a piece of skin, the ribs over the heart broken and bared of flesh, and the muscles at the breast torn into long strips, which were interlaced by their recoil from the dragging of the shot. As the soldiers placed him in a blanket his sword got entangled, and the hilt entering the wound, Captain Hardinge, a staff officer who was near, attempted to take it off, but the dying man stopped him, saying, 'It is as well as it is; I had rather it should go out of the field with me,' and in that manner so becoming to a soldier, Moore was borne from the field.[3]

As soon as it was dark we lighted our fires as if we were going to remain for the night, but afterwards began to move off. On getting to the beach, we found the boats waiting for us, and immediately pushed off, but lost one another in the darkness, and some of us not knowing where to find our ships got on board the first we came to, sending back the boats for others who were waiting for them. Here we had no sea stock but were provided with the usual ship rations, which in those days were of the worst description. As soon as the enemy found that we had embarked, they brought a battery of guns to play on us, and as the consequences of a raking shot in our crowded state would be very bad, we made our captain cut his cable.

While passing through the Bay of Biscay one of the guns on the quarter deck broke loose, and coming against the skylight broke all the glass, Which came down to us in the cabin as we lay about the floor; fortunately the gun was secured before it could follow the glass. The voyage was not a long one; the captain supposing he was going on shore at Beachy Head, cast anchor, when, to our agreeable surprise we found ourselves in the morning alongside the flag-ship, at Spithead, the commander of which received the first intelligence of the battle of Corunna from Captain Sparks, of the 51st, who had come in the same ship as myself.

3. *Napier*, vol. 1, page 490.

The remainder of the fleet having arrived, I went on board our headquarter ship, and having got some money from the paymaster, I went to an hotel in Portsmouth, purchasing some articles of clothing on my way. There I went into a bed-chamber, and having procured a large tub of water, and throwing all the clothes I had worn from the commencement of the retreat out of the window, I washed myself, and putting on the new clothes experienced a sensation of comfort, not easily described. Having ordered a beef-steak for dinner, a comrade, who shared it with me, was very angry at not having oyster sauce! Our troubles, however, were not all over, as, the day after our arrival, one of our men went into his berth and died. We were ordered to Ramsgate to disembark, before we reached it there were five hundred ill in Typhus fever. An hospital was formed at Ramsgate for our reception, and the remainder going on to Deal, were with few exceptions attacked with some disease. The virulence of this disease was such, that though there were sixteen medical attendants, they were, at one time, all seized with it, except one, and when some of the others returned to duty, he also was attacked, so that not one escaped. On one day there were 30 deaths reported. While my brother, another sub, and myself, were detached in charge of the sick at Ramsgate, we were invited to dine at the mess of a Welsh Regiment, who, acting on the hospitality of those days, locked the door and kept us drinking bumper toasts till there was not a sober man in the room. Not finding any pleasure in this, I watched my opportunity, and my two neighbours, right and left, having fallen under the table, and a waiter who came in with a fresh supply of wine, having left the door open for a few minutes, I made my escape to the first bedroom I could find, and throwing myself on the bed, remained there till morning. The regiment messed at the inn.

CHAPTER 2

The Peninsula Again

The 1st Battalion of the 52nd having been completed to one thousand men, it was dispatched to the Peninsula, and the 2nd Battalion, which I had joined as a lieutenant, was sent on the Walcheren expedition, which brings only two things to my recollection—the officers having to provide themselves with knapsacks, calculated to hold twenty-five pounds weight, and the fever which attacked us at its termination.

On re-embarking we all appeared in perfect health; yet, in the course of twenty-four hours, the greater part of the battalion were in a state of delirium. I amongst the rest, found myself at Shorncliffe, having been given over, and reduced to such a state that my nearest friends would hardly know me.

The ague, which succeeds the Walcheren fever attacked me every third day, at the same hour, each fit commenced with a great depression and sense of uneasiness—the nails became blue, and a cold feel succeeded by violent shivering, which continued a considerable time, when, the animal heat returning, became equally violent in the other extreme, till a profuse perspiration gave it vent, leaving me very weak, indeed, and I barely recovered my natural strength when the next came on. The hour of its attack was at first three o'clock, but when I began to recover, it gradually got later, till I got into another day, and at last ceased. As my dinner hour was five o'clock, when I began to pass it, and I had sat down with the expectation of being able to eat it, the fit would commence, and I was obliged to rise from the table without tasting a morsel. The treatment for ague at this time was large quantities of bark, the extract of quinine not being in use.

We embarked this time on board the *Superb,* a seventy-four. The voyage was remarkable for heavy gales, in which we had our three topmasts carried away, and I saw the Bay of Biscay in all its glory; one moment looking on the deck of a neighbouring line of battle-ship, the next looking up at her keel.

In replacing a top gallant mast, the hawser broke, when it came down by the run; touching one of our men in the forehead; the wound made appeared very small, not being more than an inch long and no breadth; there was an immense flow of blood from it, but the man was dead when it appeared that the skull was split in two. The 1st Battalion had again landed in Portugal, and after the celebrated march of 62 miles in 26 hours, arriving in time to take the out-post duty at the close of the battle of Talavera, from whence they covered the retreat before Massena's overwhelming force, taking a prominent part in the repulse at Busaco and in the defence of the celebrated lines of Torres Vedras, by which Massena lost 5 months and was finally obliged to retreat before its defenders. We arrived in Lisbon in time to join the advance after Massena's retreating army. We joined the light division, being brigaded with our 1st Battalion, some companies of the 95th Rifles, and a battalion of Caçadores.

As we advanced after Massena's retreating army we were eye witnesses of the dreadful consequences of war. Independent of the fighting part of the business, houses in ruin, some burnt with their inhabitants in them, those that could, having fled. England may be thankful at having escaped invasion by meeting the enemy at a distance. The 2nd Battalion was not actively engaged till the combat of Sabugal, 3rd April, 1811.

It was brought on by mistake, Lord Wellington's intention being to turn the enemy's left; but the officer in temporary command of the division did not sufficiently explain the order to the Brigadiers, and our first brigade was misled by a staff officer to take the bull by the horns and attack a *corps d'armee* which occupied a strong position, moreover the General had carried off the cavalry which should have been ready to give us their assistance. Hearing the first brigade under Sir Sidney Beckwith engaged, our brigade returned to their support. The 1st Battalion arrived just in time to save them and capture a howitzer. It was taken by my brother's company from the enemy. The enemy made several desperate attempts to retake it from my brother, who, with two other companies of the 52nd, held their ground and the howitzer by lining a walk in its rear. We came up on the right of the 1st Battalion, which had been waging an unequal battle with a powerful adversary. We advanced in line, being received by a heavy cannonade and volleys of musketry which we returned with interest, the enemy retreating before us. I take this occasion to point out the advantage derived from the percussion caps now in use. A heavy downfall of rain occurring in the middle of our advance, the firing on both sides ceased on the instant—not a musket would go off. Notwithstanding the deficiencies we laboured under, a volley from the 52nd was a tremendous visitation. The companies under my brother's immediate orders did great execution on the French, who endeavoured to wrest the captured howitzer from them. The individual firing was singularly good. Two instances occur to me. At Fuentes d'Onor an officer's servant, riding a runaway horse, galloped through our chain of sentries, who, supposing that he was deserting to the enemy, then not many yards distant, fired at him and knocked him off the horse. Another instance was after the battle of Salamanca, when Sir Stapleton Cotton, coming in from the front, did not hear the sentry's challenge and continued to advance, on which the sentry fired and shot him through the leg. Such was not the practice of the army, as I may safely say that not one shot in a hundred told. Sir John Moore's system of raising the musket from the *rest*, instead of letting it fall from the *present*, I believe to be the cause of this surprising difference. The double sight might have some effect but I do not think it was much used, On the evening of the combat I went to my brother's quarters at Sabugal, and found him at his mess partaking of a ham cut off the howitzer so much talked about.

Having had some correspondence in the *Naval and Military Gazette* on the subject of this howitzer, relative to the mistake which occurred in the Duke's dispatch founded on Sir Sidney Beckwith's report, taking credit to his brigade for its capture, it drew forth the following remarks from Major-General W. Napier in the *Gazette* of the 28th June, 1845, which appeal having remained unanswered to the present moment, we may consider the claims of the 52nd to be acknowledged, which they were, at the time, by Captain W. C. Madden, late of the 43rd, who is now a clergyman in the Church of England:

I was lying wounded in the rear at the time the combat of Sabugal was fought, and I am, of course, entirely dependent on my authorities; but I call upon the officers of the 43rd who still live, upon those of the Riflemen, of the artillery, of the staff, to declare whether the 43rd took the howitzer and lost it again, or 'gallantly gained and preserved it,' as the Duke of Wellington said in his dispatch. I do not mean to say that the fire of the artillery and some of the rifles did not contribute to the first gaining and then keeping of the howitzer; but I maintain, in opposition to Colonel Gurwood, as confidently as a man who was not an eye-witness can be allowed to do, the following propositions:

1st—That the howitzer was taken by the 43rd in a charge to its front.

2nd—That it remained on the spot where it was taken under the fire of the 43rd until the French retreated entirely; and, consequently, that the 43rd never lost the howitzer.

3rd—That the 43rd Regiment never turned during the day, though at one time two companies on the left, being overpowered with numbers, shifted to gain advantageous ground, as their great knowledge of war and their cool intrepidity dictated.

There are plenty of officers who can respond to the call I make, and some of them I feel will do so. Colonel Belson, of the Artillery, General Sir A. Cameron, formerly of the Rifles, General Brown, the Dep. Adjutant-General Duffy, General J. Considine, Assistant-Inspector General Gilhurst, Colonel Patrickson, General J. Ferguson, Colonel Dazell, Sir G. Houlton, Major Hopkins, were all present at the battle in a position to know the facts. Many others have gone to their last home since my last volume was published; but if those I have mentioned come forward, and do not corroborate the Duke's dispatch, and what I have said, I have nothing more to offer; and the 43rd must bear the stigma of having, for thirty years, received and rejoiced in honour which belonged to others.

In answer to Major-General Napier's first proposition, there is no evidence given by the 43rd of their ever having taken the howitzer. To his second proposition, the evidence to follow from Lieutenant-Colonel Gurwood and Lieutenant O'Hara will show that what he claims for the 43rd really belongs to the 52nd. His third proposition it is not necessary to answer. Lieutenant Gurwood says:

I was acting adjutant at the time, and am competent to corroborate, from my recollection, the facts stated in the dispatch, to, which I was witness—*viz.*, that the first brigade, under Colonel Beckwith, having advanced from the ground on which they had formed in line for attack, drove the enemy and might have taken from them a howitzer; but the brigade was overpowered and driven back, (having lost the howitzer,) to the ground of their first formation, when they were joined by the 2nd brigade, which formed on the flank of the 43rd. The whole then advanced under the command of Colonel Beckwith, assisted by Colonel Mellish, of the H. H. G. staff of the division. The 52nd passed the enclosure and the howitzer was recovered from the enemy who endeavoured to carry it off. The left centre of the 52nd on its advance came up to the howitzer being without horses at some distance in front of the enclosure; but immediately afterwards a fresh column of the enemy, supported by cavalry, charged the two regiments which were broken. The 52nd took refuge in the enclosure, when Captain Dobbs rallied his company and others and lined that part of the wall immediately opposite the howitzer (not a hundred yards from it), the remaining part of the battalion, under Colonel Ross, defending the other side of the enclosure, and in the act of jumping the wall my horse was shot by one of the enemy's hussars that came up to, and passed the gun, and both fell inside the enclosure, the horse being killed. By the fire from this part of the wall the enemy were prevented from taking away the howitzer—this a second time abandoned after its capture. A sharp fire was kept up on the French cavalry, which were driven back or destroyed; and the 52nd again advanced from the enclosure upon the enemy's infantry. Lieutenant O'Hara had cut away a ham which hung from the axle tree of the howitzer.

Memorandum on the affair at Sabugal by Colonel O'Hara, late 88th Regiment:

Castle Taylor
Ardiaham
Galway
22nd May, 1843
I must protest against the statement in Colonel W. Napier's justification (6th vol. page 13) in reply to Colonel Gurwood's annotation in the dispatches of the Duke of Wellington. (8th vol. page 557) relative to the capture of the howitzer at the affair of Sabugal. I was Lieutenant of the 1st Battalion, 52nd Regiment, in the company command-

ed by the present Colonel (then Lieut. Love) both at the Bridge of Manalva and at Sabugal; and now, after a lapse of so many years, I can recollect facts, I trust quite sufficient to establish the correctness of Colonel Gurwood's statement. We (the 52nd) advanced in line across a ravine towards the enemy in a position on some high ground opposite to us. We had nearly reached the height, when I made a rush with part of Dobbs' company, and took a large-sized howitzer. A considerable body of French cavalry were posted below the height, and were, at first, unobserved by us. We retired to a stone enclosure which fortunately was very close (about a 100 yards distant.) We then with the remainder of the regiment, which had been under cover, threw a most destructive fire on the enemy, who retired with great loss and abandoned the gun. I beg briefly to add that I cut off the howitzer a ham and some spirits, which I gave to a soldier to take care of, and whose name I remember to this day.

Lord Wellington concludes his despatch in these words:

Although the operations of this day were, by unavoidable accidents, not performed in the manner which I intended they should, I consider the action fought by the light division, by Colonel Beckwith's brigade principally, with the whole of the 2nd corps, to be one of the most glorious that British troops were ever engaged in.

And in reference to the same subject Lord Wellington's letter to Marshal Beresford, dated 4th April[1] written previous to the despatches which states:

The French then seeing how weak that body was that passed, attempted to drive them down to the Coa, and then oblige the 43rd to turn. They rallied again, however, and beat in the French, but were attacked by fresh troops and cavalry, and were obliged to retire, but formed again and beat back the enemy, and to be charged and attacked

1. See *Despatches, new edition*, vol. 4., p. 723.

again in the same manner and beat back. They formed again, moved forward upon the enemy, and established themselves on the top of the hill in an enclosure, and here they beat off the enemy. The contest was latterly entirely for the howitzer, which was taken and retaken twice, and at last remained in our hands.

From the above facts, it must appear that the 52nd bore a more prominent part in the contest than they got credit for in the dispatch, having taken and retaken the howitzer, which the Duke states to be the principal part of the contest. The distance from the scene prevented him from distinguishing which regiment was in the enclosure.

As my expression of a ham being cut off a howitzer seems to have puzzled some of my friends, it may be well to state that artillery officers as well as infantry officers are glad to attend to their mess comforts, and if they happen to meet with a ham, or any article of that nature, they would suspend it from part of the gun carriage till it could be disposed of. While speaking of mess comforts, I have to state that there were many articles which we only procure from sutlers, who found it their interest in bringing them up from the nearest sea-ports, for which articles they got great prices. Tea, ale, porter, soda water, cheese, &c, &c. Speaking of soda water— which I had no taste for—many thought a great luxury. The prices were 2s. 6d. a bottle; and those who had half-crowns to spare, and were fond of it, would call for a bottle of it and drink it off in great glee. On one occasion a Portuguese officer thought that it must be something delightful, so he called for one and drank it off; but when he got the taste of it, he threw down his half-crown and ran out of the shop. In Spain tea was used as a medicine and was only sold in apothecaries' shops. Potatoes sold for 6d a pound. Money being generally scarce we were obliged to live on our daily rations, which consisted of a pound of biscuits or a pound and a half of soft bread, with one pound of beef,—salt or fresh—or a pound of salt pork. The fresh beef was nearly all skin and bone. I seldom got sufficient to satisfy my hunger; and yet, when we got to the Pyrenees, I was in such good condition that my friends used to call me the *porpoise*.

In speaking of our old muskets I forgot to remark the inferior nature of the flints, which were often had, so that after a volley nearly one-fourth part had missed fire.

On the 25th of April, 1811, Massena, having collected his army at Ciudad Rodrigo, for the relief of Almeida, made an attack on our picquet at the bridge of Marialva on the Azava with a large force of cavalry and infantry. There was a ford a short distance below the bridge, and the company on outlying picquet had a subdivision at each point. Both passages were important, but the ford was considered more so than the other, consequently the captain remained at the ford and the other subdivision was under the command of his lieutenant. The relieving picquet always arrived an hour before daylight, both picquets remaining under arms till the daylight enabled them to ascertain there was no enemy in. On the 23rd of April the company under my brother, Captain Joseph Dobbs, being the relieving one, was under arms with the old picquet, also a company of the 52nd my brother being in command of all who were stationed at the ford and bridge. Just as daylight appeared he heard a heavy firing at the bridge, and having ascertained that the ford was not passable in consequence of a heavy fall of rain taking place during the night, he left a corporal and three men to watch it, and dashed off with the remainder to the bridge. He arrived most opportunely, the enemy having forced the passage, and he having seen the state of affairs whilst coming over the height above the bridge, charged down on the enemy, who, supposing that he was only the advance of a large force gave way and recrossed the bridge, on which my brother established his men amongst the rocks on our side of the bridge; keeping up. such a fire that the enemy were unable to force the passage a second time. Their manner of advance was rather singular—a drummer led the company, beating what we had nicknamed *Old Trousers*; as long as he survived they continued to advance, but so soon as he fell they immediately turned tail and ran back, when they had to go over the same process for another attack. This continued for a considerable length of time until we, the 1st and 2nd battalions of the 52nd were able to come to the relief of the picquet, when the enemy retired to their main body at Ciudad Rodrigo. It may be supposed how much my brother exposed himself, when I state that he had a shot through his cap, another through his jacket, another cut the flap of his trousers across, and another on the blade of his sabre, now in my possession.

If the enemy had succeeded in their attack on the bridge, much mischief might have been done, as all our Horse Artillery's horses were out foraging, and their cavalry would have gone into our quarters at Gallegos, before we were prepared to receive them. According to Napier's account, the attacking force consisted of two thousand infantry, and a squadron of cavalry.

The battle of Fuentes d'Onor lasted from the 5th to the 6th May, 1811. On the morning of the first days fighting the 7th division occupied some heights at the extreme right of the position, the Light Division a plain on their left, and a wood, which communicated with the division which occupied Fuentes d'Onor. The enemy attacked the 7th Division in the morning, and brought five thousand cavalry to bear on our small body of cavalry immediately in front, which was obliged to retire. We were somewhat startled by Sir Sydney Beckwith, riding up, exclaiming "they're in among you, they're in among you!" and presently we saw the troop of Horse Artillery, with their guns, surrounded by the enemy, but gallantly fighting their way out. With the most perfect coolness the three battalions 1st of the 43rd and 1st and 2nd of the 52nd, formed an echelon of squares which covered the retreat of our Horse Artillery. Lord Wellington having determined on a change of position, the 7th Division were ordered to retire, and. we had to do the same over the plain, to the new position; this was done by alternate squares, under a heavy cannonade, the balls sometimes hopping in and out of the square. The distance was about three miles, and marching in square a most difficult operation, as if the correct line is not kept by the front and rear faces, or the sides in file marching not looked up or well covered, the square must be broken. In the evening of the second day of the battle we were ordered into the town, and I had one of the out-lying picquets. A few hours before daylight I heard a rolling of wheels, but could not tell whether the enemy was retiring or bringing up more artillery. As our sentries were on one side of a narrow stream, and the enemy's on the other, it was not easy for them to get off without being perceived, but they managed it thus: when relieving sentries, they placed a straw figure, with a French cap on its head, and a pole like the barrel of a musket standing on its side. Not wishing to create a false alarm, it was some time before I could ascertain the truth, but at once reported my suspicions to headquarters, I take this opportunity of mentioning the terms on which we were with the enemy, when not engaged. Our side of the stream was so steep that we could not get at the water, while theirs was easy of access; on making friendly signals to them, they filled our wooden canteens for us—we throwing them over, and they returning them filled.

In the middle of June, 1811, Marmont having crossed the Tagus, to co-operate with Soult in the relief of the second siege of Badajos, we also crossed the Tagus by the Pontoon Bridge at Vilha Velha, to support the besiegers. While occupying a bivouac behind a wooded ridge, between Campo Major and the Caya, one of those accidents occurred which are so frequent in hot countries. The whole surface was covered with long dry grass, and some of the troops having lit their fires to windward, in a few moments it took fire, and the flames quickly spread in every direction, setting fire to the huts, and in many instances blowing up the men's pouches. The 95th suffered most.

This accident reminds me of the depopulated state of Spain, which causes this extent of wilderness; the inhabitants live in villages, usually about five leagues apart, having a circle of uncultivated land around them, generally occupied by woods, which shelter large packs of wolves. One instance of the boldness of these wolves occurs to me, but at this distance of time, I cannot remember at which of the villages it happened. A flock of sheep collected during the night, on the ground used for thrashing out corn, was attacked by a large pack of wolves; the alarm was given, and natives and soldiers quickly turned out, the former directing our movements. Our plan was to form a line of sharp-shooters under the brow of a hill, and then to make an arc of a circle round the cover in which the wolves had taken shelter, making the line of sharp-shooters its chord; the circle gradually closing in, the wolves passed over the heights, and received the fire of our sharp-shooters. In this way eleven of them were killed, to the great delight of the shepherds. On second thoughts, I think the village was Casellos de Flores, it was after Marmont had relieved Rodrigo, and we had been forced to retire to the Coa, being, while quartered there orderly officer of the day, it was part of my duty to visit our out-lying picquet which was stationed in a thick wood at some distance from the village, my visit was made about midnight. While passing through the wood, the wolves were howling in every direction, and when I got to the picquet I found they had let their fire get very low, but on hearing their flying sentries challenge, some of them jumped up and stirred it, when a rush of wolves escaping took place. I do not remember an instance of their attacking live men, with the exception of an orderly dragoon, who got drunk and lay on the ground in a state of helplessness, he was killed and eaten by them, with the exception of his feet, which were preserved by his boots. I have seen horses and cows with the flesh torn off their hind quarters still alive, only the bones of others remaining, and on one occasion I found the remains of a brother officer (who was hastily buried with the men's bayonets in our retreat) torn up by them, when a few months afterwards we passed it in advance, we only ascertained it by a piece of his shirt-tail which had a mark on it, and that not his own, but a friend's who had been killed, and whose baggage was handed over to him.

The inhabitants cultivate wheat and Indian corn in a circle, extending for about a mile round each village. The wheat, when ripe, is threshed by oxen, which are fastened by a long pole, to a post which turns with them, and keeps them in their places, as they are driven round, treading out the corn. Their ploughs are wooden ones, and barely scrape the ground; their bullock carts are equally rough, and as they never grease their axles they make a disagreeable creaking noise. The bullocks are harnessed to their work by a heavy piece of wood laid on their necks and lashed to their horns, by which the poor animals suffer dreadfully, particularly in hot weather. Their sheep, oxen, and pigs are under charge of herds, who keep dogs to assist in watching them in the uncultivated waste land. Pigs are in the best condition when the acorns are ripe; they are driven into woods, and brought home at night. It is an amusing sight to see them dismissed in the evening at the entrance of the village, every one running to its own home. They make a rush like a charge of cavalry, and if the passage is narrow, it is rather dangerous to meet them. The houses in the Spanish villages consist of a kitchen, in which all the family sit, and several sleeping apartments. The kitchen is the only room which contains a chimney; the window's have no sashes, and are closed by wooden shutters. The roofs are covered with tiles. These houses are very pleasant in summer, but most uncomfortable in winter. When billeted on them in this season, (as it would not do for an officer to sit in the kitchen) we had to adopt some means of making the rooms we occupied more comfortable. We used to run up a wall at one of the corners, leaving room for a fire at the bottom, and breaking a hole out of the top of the chimney; this was a great annoyance to the landlords, and as the chimneys generally smoked, was not particularly comfortable for his tenants; the following scene occurred in consequence:

> Captain Currie, of the 52nd, was sitting over his fire, which smoked very much; the landlord perceiving this, came in and sat down, watching the captain, who being a very patient man, sat very quietly without showing his annoyance. The landlord on this grew wild, and jumping up, exclaimed, "If you can stand fire as well as you stand smoke, you are one of the best soldiers in His Britannic Majesty's army."

It must be remembered that wood is the fuel used, and that it is laid on the ground. In the better class of houses, charcoal is used in a round brass pan, which fits into a wooden frame, on which seats can be placed. There are some parts of the country where there is no wood, and the inhabitants are obliged to use straw. We found this a great hardship when we had to bivouac, having no shelter from the sun by day, nor from the heavy dew by night, except our blankets, until there were four tents served out to each company, one for the officers, and three for the men. Our manner of cooking was adapted to our circumstances; one servant went for wood, another for water, and the third, or one of ourselves, prepared what we had to cook. By this division of labour the work was soon accomplished. Short as it was, however, I have been disturbed in it by the enemy's movements, and on one occasion had to throw out the soup, and pack up the meat three times before it was dressed; as to the last water, it could not be called soup.

Being unable to procure cow's milk, and goat's milk being very scarce, we found it a great comfort to have our own goats. We had several to each company, and they became so tame, that we found them very troublesome; they would occupy our beds, and follow us about when we did not want them. The officers of each company messed together, and had a boy to drive the goats. While on the subject of mess matters, I may mention an accident which gave me some annoyance, but which was rather an amusement to my comrades. We were engaged in preparing a dish which required pepper, and had got some red-pepper pods for the purpose of seasoning it. Having taken one in my hand, I happened to touch my eyes and lips with my fingers, when both were set smarting in a way that drove me wild.

Our Commissariat, although greatly improved by Lord Wellington's regulations, was frequently unable to meet our necessities from want of money, and means of transport. We were frequently days without bread or salt; and the draught bullocks likely to die, were killed and served out for rations. Our pay being in arrears, we had no money to purchase what we might otherwise have procured from the natives.

It may be interesting to show the manner in which we got under arms. The old plan was by bugle calls by day, and an alarm by night in the same way; but now the most perfect silence was preserved. The commander of the division had an orderly from each brigade, who carried the order to the Brigadier, who again had an orderly from each regiment, and the regimental commander had an orderly from each company; the sergeants were obliged to get the roll of the company by heart, so that when called out at night they did not require a light for the purpose. Although these matters may appear trifling, yet they conduced greatly to the efficiency of the Light Division, of whom the Duke of Wellington was heard to say, that he gave them an order overnight, for a dangerous service, and on the following morning the work was done, and the division on parade, as if nothing had happened. Another cause of efficiency was Crawford's system of not drinking on the march, which was observed by all the old soldiers, and prevented the falling out of the ranks, which may generally be observed in younger ones.

Breaking up from the Caya on the 21st July, we recrossed the Tagus in the beginning of August. In September the Light Division was posted on the Vadilla, and were employed making fascines and gabions for the siege of Rodrigo. Shortly after this the famous comet made its appearance; it was very fine, but I consider that of 1858 finer.

The Light Division being engaged in the distant investment of Ciudad Rodrigo, were cut off from the rest of the army by the advance of the enemy for its relief. The latter having effected their purpose, crossed the Aguada on the 25th of September, and attacked our forces at Elbedon, by which movement they got into our rear, and our division had to work round their flank to rejoin the main body. The baggage had to make a still greater detour through the woods, and under the mountain. Our baggage guard consisted of the two batmen belonging to each company, with some others belonging to the staff, an officer of each battalion having the command. The tail of each company's mules being tied to its follower were led by one of the batmen, the other being left free to act as circumstances might require. Having the baggage guard on this occasion, while passing through the wood after nightfall, I met two officers wearing cocked hats and blue frock coats, and supposing them to be Frenchmen, I called for one or two of the batmen, and seized the bridle of one of the horses. I found, however, that my prisoners were Major O'Kelly of the 11th and another officer who were out reconnoitring. About two years after this, I was crossing the Crown mountain, on my way to join the 5th Caçadores at the siege of St. Sebastian, and was leading my horse down the mountain, when I was overtaken by a field officer, who was also leading his horse. We entered into conversation, and after some time he said, "I have heard your voice before;" I replied that I had no recollection of having ever met him. He said, "Do you remember taking me prisoner in a wood near the Vadilla, and calling out to your men, 'Come here one or two of you'?" Major O'Kelly was perfect in all the languages spoken in the Peninsula, and was particularly adapted to the service in which I first met him. No one could guess to what nation he belonged. After my encounter with Major O'Kelly we came to an extensive bivouac, and going forward with a file of men to reconnoitre, to our surprise we were allowed to approach close to one of their fires without challenge, when we heard the greatest confusion of language spoken. These were men in charge of Commissariat and Ordnance stores, &c.; they were composed of Portuguese, Spaniards, Germans, and English, who were in the same predicament as ourselves. The next day we rejoined the army at Fuente Guinalda, having found that the enemy had a few hours previously been on the ground we had marched over.

Lord Wellington having retired to Nava de Vere during the night our chaplain remaining after the troops, was taken by the enemy, and after a few days was sent back as a non-combatant, but such articles of his baggage as were found useful retained.

This leads me to remark, that during the whole period of my foreign service in the Peninsula, Sweden or Walcheren, the regiment was never once assembled for Divine Service, nor could the Lord's day be distinguished from week days.

Some time after Massena's retreat, an officer, son of an eminent dentist in Dublin, being left in the rear, in charge of sick and wounded, was in the habit of visiting them for the purpose of reading the scriptures, or speaking to them on religious subjects; his conduct was immediately reported to Lord Wellington, with a request that he might be reprimanded. His Lordship's reply was that he did not see how he could interfere, so long as he did not neglect his own duty. At this time it was supposed that a Christian must necessarily be a milksop and a coward, and was looked upon with great contempt.

As soon as the French retired the troops were quartered in the villages, on the left bank of the Aguada, close to Rodrigo, we were quartered in Elbedon.

In crossing the Aguada to take our tour of duty in the siege of Ciudad Rodrigo, we had to ford it, the water being up to our hips; and as there was a heavy hoar frost during the whole period of the siege, and we lay on the bare ground for six hours during the night, with only a single blanket to cover us, we were sufficiently cooled; our blankets after the night were stiff enough to stand upright. About this time, I had risen to the head of the 2nd Battalion Lieutenants, and was transferred to the 1st Battalion as Junior Lieutenant. I was attached to my brother's Company.

On the 8th of January, 1812, the first night of the siege, the company was engaged with Sir John Colborne in storming the redoubt of St. Francisco; his orders were so plain that no man could mistake his post. The redoubt was attacked on all sides at once, and I believe every man of its garrison could be accounted for as killed or prisoner. As soon as it was carried I was telling off the company on the glacis, when Sir John (now Lord Seaton) expressed his satisfaction at my conduct to my brother. After having carried it we advanced to a watercourse just under the walls, to prevent a sortie by the enemy on our working party, who were breaking ground on a line with the redoubt we had taken; the French had their breaching batteries on this spot when they were taking it from the Spaniards.

As soon as the enemy ascertained that the redoubt was in our possession, they opened a tremendous fire of shot and shell on it, all of which passed over our heads. We lay there till daylight, when we were obliged to retire to a more covered position.

The duty for the twenty-four hours was, six hours trenches and six hours out of them, alternately. The trench duty was six hours working and six hours covering, and then we had our hip-bath in the Aguada on our return to quarters at Elbedon.

On the last day of the siege, the 19th January, 1812, the four divisions being collected for the assault, my brother, being the second senior captain with the Regiment, claimed the right of leading the column; the Regimental order being, the senior Captain's Company on the right, the next in order on the left of the Battalion, and so on, and the order of attack being "Left in front;" this placed him by the side of General Vandeleur and Lieutenant Colonel Colborne, On their reaching the head of the breach there was a volley from their flank which the General and Lieutenant Colonel received in their shoulders and which cost my poor brother his life.

We and the 43rd moved up the breach in sections of threes, my post was in rear of the company. The orders were to wheel to the left after mounting the breach, and so to compass the ramparts on its right, while the 43rd did the same to its left, which brought them into the rear of the defenders of the large breach.

When I got to the head of the breach, I found Colonel Colborne, although wounded, directing the head of the column, with which I passed on, not knowing my poor brother's fate till morning.

After the siege of Rodrigo, we were sent into winter quarters, and everything appeared to be at a standstill. Lord Wellington's hounds were sent out to the front, as if he was satisfied with what had been done, and only thought of his amusement. The French generals who had failed in the relief of Rodrigo, also took up their winter quarters, not suspecting any further movement on our part. But Lord Wellington was hard at work getting up his siege train by the Tagus, and suddenly moved across that river by the bridge of Vilha Velha. The siege train had been lying at Elvas, where the necessary fascines and gabions had also been prepared.

About this time I cut my *wisdom teeth*, the torture was very great, and my bed very hard, the bedstead being a door, and the bedding a cloak and blanket, and the pillow my servant's knapsack.

CHAPTER 3

Storming Badajoz

Arriving at Badajos on the 17th of March, 1812, we broke ground after nightfall; A heavy fall of rain, high wind, and the nature of the ground, which was a deep bed of clay, prevented the enemy in Fort Pecurina from hearing or seeing us, although only about one hundred and sixty yards distant. At Ciudad Rodrigo, the surface being gravel, every blow of the pickaxe was heard, and the sparks of fire from the gravel were seen; at Badajos, on the other hand, the constant rain caused the trenches to become beds of mud.

The enemy's shell's at Rodrigo were more destructive than at Badajos, the surface being hard, the shells did not sink into the ground, consequently fell in all directions, while at Badajos, they sank into the clay, and you could lie quite close to them without danger, the splinters flying upwards. To persons who have not read on the subject it may be well to state that, in every battery there is a person on the look out, who calls out at every discharge from the enemy, ball or shell, as it may be; when the former each person covers himself behind the parapet; if the latter, it was watched as it took its course through the air till it fell; if close, you fell flat on the ground, till it exploded; if at a distance, you had to take your chance.

We had, however, the advantage of being within half an hour's march of our tents; but even the tents in heavy rain were anything but comfortable, and besides, were within range of the enemy's guns. Our camp was to the left of the inundation, which ran between our trenches and the town.

In the storming of Fort Pecurina, which was done by the 3rd Division, and some of our Division, Captain Madden of the 52nd, (who had been out shooting, and had a shooting jacket on) followed the stormers into the fort. Here he became exposed to the fire of both sides, as neither could tell what he was; however he escaped unhurt. He was under the impression that he was invulnerable, but unfortunately for his theory, he was killed in storming the breaches on the last night of the siege. His brother of the 43rd was supposed to be mortally wounded in the same attack. On this occasion, for the first time, I heard a complaint of the want of the Sacred Scriptures; there was not a copy to be found amongst us. I am happy to say, that in this respect the state of things is altered.

On the opening of one of our first counter-batteries, I happened to be in the covering party, and occupied a trench in its front, running parallel to the battery; the enemy opened a tremendous fire on it, and in a short time dismounted several guns and disabled others. On this a message came to us requesting that we would endeavour to stop the enemy's fire. Accordingly we opened fire on their embrasures, and the effect of the fire was such, that in about twenty minutes they had to stop them with gabions. Some of the shots struck the sides and glanced right and left—others went right through the centre, so that the gunners could not stand to their guns. I do not remember our distance from the walls, but the trench ran along the front of the batteries, about fifty yards nearer to the walls.

On the 6th April the fourth and Light Divisions got under arms at sunset, and as soon as it was dark moved along the left bank of the stream, and inundation to the attack of the three breaches. The left hand one was in the face of the bastion and impracticable, the centre and large one, in the curtain, and right hand one in the flank of the next bastion. The centre and right hand ones were perpendicular; Philipon, having had the rubbish cleared away from the breaches every night, which could not be prevented, as our breaching batteries from their distance could not be brought to bear on the wall lower than the glacis. The head of the breaches after our batteries had stopped for the night were enclosed by a *chevaux de frize* of sword blades, fastened by chains and bags of old iron, barrels full of nails, and boards with nails sticking out of them. The former were prepared to roll down on the stormers, and the latter to lie flat on the breach. Shells were ranged along the parapet and howitzers, and mortars placed so as to throw fire balls into the ditch. The head of each breach and the connecting parapet were lined with men, those at the breaches having fresh loaded muskets handed to them in exchange for those discharged, beside a ball cartridge, each musket contained a round piece of wood with eight slugs stuck into eight holes, which on the discharge were separated like a discharge of grape, supposing the breaches carried. A deep ditch, defended by a breast-work, would have to be carried; the ditch appeared to me to be 24 feet deep, and in front of the curtain was an unfinished ravelin. The inundation flooded the ditch up to the ravelin, and opposite the left hand breach its depth exceeded six or seven feet. Such was the defence we had to encounter, our descent into the ditch was effected by ladders, from ignorance of the depth of water opposite the left hand breach, several of the ladders were placed in it, and the consequence was, a number of men were drowned in it. Our orders were, not to fire a shot, and, if I recollect right, the men were not permitted to load. To obviate this defenceless state a number of rifle men were placed on the glacis to fire over our heads till we could reach the breaches. As I was attached to one of the rear companies, I had an opportunity of seeing the commencement of the assault and defence. As soon as the head of the column was discovered, the enemy opened on us with shot, shell, and musketry, first having ascertained our whereabouts by fire balls; but when the ditch became crowded with men, the shells on the parapet were lighted and thrown over, fire balls were thrown into the ditch, so that every man could be seen and exposed to a murderous fire of musketry. The ladder I descended was at the edge of the inundation, and I got into about a foot of water at first. I turned to my right, and finding the water get deeper, I retraced my steps, and came to the unfinished ravelin (which I fancied to be one of the breaches), and shouting to the men to come on, found our mistake. As no impression could be made on the breach, every man mounting being swept down, and the whole ditch crowded with men, dead and alive, we remained under fire for two hours, till Lord Wellington sent word that the Castle was taken, and ordered the men out of the ditch to reform, which was done in a gravel-pit close to the glacis; and as numbers had gone off with wounded men to the hospital tents, I was sent to bring them back. Having done so, at day light, we were marching to the breaches, and having succeeded in removing, the obstruction made good our entrance. The scene in the ditch was dreadful, and as we mounted the breach we met some prisoners coming out. One of them, an officer, who, looking on the dead bodies lying before him, smiled at them, which so enraged one of our men, that he knocked him down.

The siege of Badajos cost us more men and officers than any other siege or action we were engaged in. There were seven captains killed or wounded in the ditch—three of them killed, and one died of his wound; twenty-two officers, and seventy non-commissioned officers and men. There were only eight officers fit for duty on the 7th April, the day after the assault.

Captain Jones, our senior captain, was one of the killed; he was a very brave and gallant officer. We had been chatting together a few hours before the storming. He was a Welshman, and had a gruff way of speaking, in addition to his native accent. Speaking of the assault he said, "I'll be a man or a mouse to-night." He commanded our hundred stormers at Rodrigo; and a short time after it was in our possession, finding a number of the soldiers in a church sitting round a fire which they had lit on the pavement (having previously ascertained that it was used as a magazine, and that a great number of barrels of powder were piled at the end of it), he immediately turned the men out, and with his own hands carefully carried out each brand, and had the door secured. At the battle of Busaco, the enemy advancing in a column of grand divisions, their right hand company came in contact with our right hand flank company, the regiment being in line; the company was commanded by Captain Jones, the captains met hand to hand, and the Frenchman was killed in the encounter.

Those who lay great stress on presentiments, will find something to unsettle this idea in the feelings of the three captains killed at Badajos. Captain Madden thought himself invulnerable, Captain Jones looked on it as a doubtful case, and Captain Poole expressed himself as going to certain death.

When we got into Badajos, through the breaches, the enemy having abandoned them, when the Castle was taken by the third divisions, it was found impossible to keep the men together, and a scene of plunder and drunkenness took place of the worst character, and it was found necessary for some time to let it take its course. I had a narrow escape from some drunken men who were following a bull through a street, as I was coming from the other end, they fired a volley at it which passed me in all directions.

Having returned to camp, the men began gradually to return, laden with plunder—some dressed as monks, others in female dresses, some as Frenchmen officers. All we could do was to keep them from going back, and they gradually returned to duty.

On the 8th April I was ordered on command, with all the

wounded that could be moved, to Elvas. On going to take charge I found the surgeon still busily employed in cutting off legs and arms, of which there was an immense heap close to the hospital tents. Surgeon Maling was a man of first class abilities in his profession; he was rather rough in his manner, but very prompt to act. I found him on this occasion with his coat off, his sleeves tucked up, his patient sketched upon a table, and the knife in his hand, and after a sweeping cut round the limb, he would take the knife between his teeth that he might have his hands free to tie up the arteries. When a case of emergency arose he would throw off his coat and tuck up his sleeves, which action gave him among the men the nickname of *Short Sleeves*. One look was sufficient to satisfy him when a man was shamming. I am proud to say we had few of this class. My orders were to deliver my charge at the hospital, formed at Elvas, and to return at once to the regiment, from which I could not be spared. Mules and bullock cars were provided for the wounded; many of them had their arms amputated on the night of the storm, and others with slight wounds preferred walking to riding, the shaking causing them greater pain than moving on their feet. I arrived late in the day, placed my charge in safety, and returned to my regiment, having escaped an attack from some brigands whom I passed in the dark. They gave me a few shots to hasten my return. I arrived before daylight, and found the battalion under orders to cross the Tagus at Vilha Velha, to put a stop to the advance of Marmont, who had entered Portugal, and was threatening Almeida and Ciudad Rodrigo, and was doing all the mischief he could in our rear. Soult was only a few marches from Badajos when it was taken in a day or two more we should have had to raise the siege.

Marmont retiring on our approach we enjoyed about two months' rest, during which time most of our wounded rejoined, and in June we began our advance on Salamanca.

From this period we found a great change for the better

in the Spaniards. We were received with shouts of long life to the English, and in the large cities the windows were crowded with beautiful females waving their handkerchiefs as we passed through the streets at our entrance. They were allowed to walk only as Spanish women can walk, on their *prados*, in full dress, being a great compliment to us and an indulgence to them.

On the 17th of June we passed the Tormes, leaving Salamanca in our rear, and having the 6th Division engaged in the siege of the French forts. On the 20th Marmont advanced to our front with four divisions and a brigade of cavalry, and on the 22nd he received three more divisions and another brigade of cavalry. These additions enabled him to make an attack on our right, which was repulsed by General Graham with the 7th division, on which the French retired about six miles. On the 27th, the forts had fallen, Marmont retreated behind the Douro followed by the British; but having obtained large reinforcements, he was again enabled to commence offensive operations, constantly out-flanking us. On the 17th July we were marching in parallel columns, at about a stone's throw from one another—it was a beautiful sight and continued for ten miles. The question was, who should arrive first at the river Guarena. We accomplished our object; when the enemy finding we had slipped through their fingers, opened a heavy cannonade on our column. The weather being very sultry, and our men suffering from thirst, they contrived to slack it by dipping their hands in the water as they marched through it. We soon got into communication with the rest of the army, who were in a strong position on the banks of the river. On the 21st of July, the enemy having crossed the Tormes between Alba de Tonnes and Huerta, we also crossed it lower down. The night was dark, and a tremendous storm of thunder, lightning and rain was raging while we passed down the bank of the river to the ground marked out for our encampment. We had been allowed four bell-tents to each company—one for the officers and three for the men; there was great difficulty in pitching them, and when pitched they afforded very poor shelter, and were blown down once or twice in the night. In the middle of the night some of the cavalry horses broke from their picquets and galloped through the camp, so that it was supposed that the enemy were. amongst us; and it was some time before it could be ascertained what was the matter.

The British position on the 22nd was two sides of a right angled triangle. We occupied the centre, and had an opportunity of seeing all the movements going forward, up to the advance of the 3rd Division and Bradford's Portuguese Brigade—to the latter of which I was afterwards attached as a captain in the 5th Caçadores. About five o'clock in the evening I was looking at the French troops who were moving towards the right, with the intention of cutting off the communication with Ciudad Rodrigo, when I exclaimed to some brother officers, with whom I was conversing, "O! that we had a division at that hill." While I was speaking the 3rd Division made its appearance from behind it, and the rout of the French army was the consequence. We were ordered to advance, and we chased the enemy till darkness prevented further pursuit. On the 23rd the enemy formed a rear-guard from the confusion which prevailed the night before; and the heavy German Cavalry, supported by the light division, commenced an active pursuit. The Germans charged the enemy's squares and broke them, on which the latter threw down their arms (which lay as if regularly grounded) and fled over the plain pursued by the Germans to whom they surrendered as they came up. It was amusing to see a single horseman riding back to us with a crowd of Frenchmen around him. It must, however, be remembered that being without arms they were exposed to a worse enemy—the Partidas—and were therefore glad to have British protection.

The effect of the battle of Barossa, won by Graham, the surprise of Almaras, by Hill, the capture of Ciudad Rodrigo,

Badajos and the forts of Salamanca, and of the battle of Salamanca, were the relief of Cadiz, and the junction of Graham's army with that of Lord Wellington, while Hill was advancing closer. The French army had been obliged to retire from the advanced positions and formed a more contracted one around the British—having Clauzel in command of the right, Joseph of the centre, and Soult of the left. The battle of Salamanca had paralysed them, and Lord Wellington advanced to Burgos on the left, and Madrid in the centre. The Light Division with Lord Wellington's main body, and Hill on the right, drove Joseph and his army before them to Madrid; which they were obliged to evacuate in the greatest confusion, leaving behind them in the retire, a garrison of two thousand men, and enormous stores—one hundred and eighty pieces of artillery, twenty thousand stand of arms, &c, all of which were surrendered without a shot. As we crossed the Guaderama we came upon the famous palace of the Escurial, which many of us took the opportunity of visiting. It was built by a Spanish king, in honour of St. Laurence, said to be martyred by being broiled on a gridiron; the outer building is a square, representing the frame of a gridiron, while there are a number of smaller buildings representing the bars of it. The building contains a residence for the Royal family, also accommodation for a number of monks, having a fine place of worship, cloisters, &c. The burial place of the Royal family is also here, its entrance is by a beautiful staircase, lined with marble, which leads to the splendid marble apartment I think eight sided, having marble coffins ranged in niches, one above the other, each containing a crowned head.

There are other apartments in this part of the building, one containing the members of the Royal family, in wooden berths like those of the cabin of a packet. The bodies are embalmed, and baked in two ovens prepared, one for the men and the other for the women. Their coffins had been opened by the French, and left exposed to view, in their full dress—I took two silk buttons off John of Austria's dress, what became of them, I cannot tell.

We arrived at Madrid on the 12th of August, 1812, and after the surrender of the Retiro our Brigade was sent to the advanced post of Gatafe, where we remained till obliged to retreat after the failure at Burgos. While we remained at Gatafe we had an invitation from the Spaniards to witness one of their bullfights at Madrid, and another from Lord Wellington to a splendid ball and supper, to which all went who could be spared. It was given in Joseph's palace, and we had some of Joseph's wine which was of the first quality.

The bullfight, I will endeavour concisely to describe, although I fear it may, prove uninteresting to most of my readers. It is held in an immense uncovered circus, surrounded by a strong barricade about four feet high, having a passage about six feet broad between it and the front seats prepared for the spectators; these are tier above tier being divided into boxes, and having a splendid one provided for Royalty, or the authority who presides. On one side of the circus there is an entrance by folding doors, and at the other an entrance from the apartment from which the bull is to enter having also folding doors. The scene commences with all the spear-men entering the circus through the door opposite the Royal box, and having saluted the person or persons representing Royalty, they retire with the exception of two; these place themselves in front of the door by which the bull is to enter, which being thrown open after a flourish of trumpets, he generally enters with a bound, having a number of pigeons which had been confined with him fluttering about his head. On seeing the vast concourse of people, he generally stops and looks about with surprise, till beholding the two horse-men motionless before him, he gives a bellow, and begins tearing the ground with his feet, and taking his aim, lowers his head and charges one of the horsemen whose spear is lowered to meet him, and when rightly directed catches him in the shoulder and turns him off. The spear can only enter about an inch into the animal, having a ball at the end which prevents its doing more. Should the horseman miss his aim the bull gets under the horse, tossing him and the rider over, and generally leaving the poor horse, when he rises, with his bowels hanging out, the man is seldom hurt. Immediately on the accident taking place, a number of men with small flags in their hands jump over the barricade into the circus, flicking them into the bull's face till he is drawn off from the horse and man, and when he runs at them they jump back into the passage between the barricade and audience. When the bulls are very active they sometimes jump over the barricade too, on which the flagmen jump into the circus, and the bull proceeds on till he comes to a door left open for the purpose and again enters the circus, the door is then shut and the flagmen jump into the passage. After several encounters with the horsemen he gets tired of attacking them, when the flagmen proceed to tease them first with the flags, only jumping over the barricade whenever he makes a rush on them that they cannot otherwise escape. When the bull is too quiet they have small darts with lighted fireworks attached, which being stuck into the animal give him great annoyance; some of the most active flagmen jump across his head and strike a couple of these darts into his neck behind his horns. After this has continued some time they retire, and the matador or killer enters the circus, armed with a long straight sword, sharp at both sides and tapering to a point in his right hand, and one of the flags in his left, he advances to the bull, whose experience and fatigue has made more cautious, and standing before him waits his attack, which at last takes place; having taken his aim first, the bull lowers his head and shuts his eyes, and makes a rush at the man, which he dexterously avoids by moving to the left, and receiving it on the flag in his left hand, which is held across his body, and with the right enters the sword above the shoulder, on which the bull impales himself and falls dead.

The entrance door is then thrown open, and two mules gaily caparisoned are driven in and fastened to the bull, dragging him out of the circus, which is then raked over and made ready for another bullfight. In this manner sixteen bulls met their death, the seventeenth was beaten with dogs, and then killed by the matador; it was the middle one of the sixteen beaten by men, eight preceded it and eight succeeded it; a number of dogs, after several being killed succeeded in pinning it, so that it could not move, when the matador killed it by running his sword through the body in different parts.

The first horse was gored with his bowels hanging out. The Spanish audience, particularly the women, called on the spearman to mount again. This struck us as an extra act of cruelty, and we cried out against it, and made such a row as prevented his doing so, and the horse was removed and a fresh one brought in.

On the 23rd of August we left Gatafe on our way to Salamanca. A little way on the Madrid side of the Guaderama Pass, and not far from the Escurial, we were halted with our arms piled, when a wild boar was started, which was the occasion of a singular state of confusion. A general attack was made on him, some of the men throwing themselves on his back, others trying to get a blow at him as he ran among the piled arms; at last a butcher got a blow at him with his axe, and struck him on the head, when he was soon dispatched.

Having joined the troops retreating from Burgos, we took the rear-guard, and commenced our retreat from Salamanca on the 15th of November, 1812.

Soult having turned our flank, we were engaged in covering the retreat of the army on the 15th and 16th of November. The forests we were passing through were occupied by numerous herds of pigs, feeding on the acorns which fell from the trees; the divisions that preceded us pursued and killed numbers of them, creating an alarm by their firing. Our men were free from blame in this matter—however they might be inclined, they were too near the enemy to attempt it. I must observe that we were here suffering from want of rations, as by a mistake the ration bullocks had been sent to the rear with the baggage.

On the 17th the division bivouacked on a hill sloping to the front, with a valley behind. While the men were folding their blankets I happened to go to the rear, and on looking into the valley saw several French dragoons riding at their leisure, I lost no time in giving the alarm; it appeared that our cavalry pickets had retired without giving us notice. During this day the enemy's cavalry were in our rear and upon our flank, and we were obliged to march in column at quarter distance, and frequently to form squares. On one occasion, General Vandeleur and his staff had to take shelter in ours. Gen. Vandeleur had never served with infantry till he got command of our brigade. And as some of the distance had been lost by some of the rear companies, when the sections wheeled up to form square, there was a gap in the square which I was putting to rights by making all the men close in by side step, this appeared to him confusion; and he returned me thanks for my exertion, which was nothing out of the common. During this day's retreat, General Paget and part of our baggage were carried off from between the head of our division and the rear of his own, the 1st division; and finally, under the fire of thirty pieces of cannon, we crossed the Huibra, and occupied an oak wood in defence of the lower fords.

In passing along the banks of this river, the French threw a number of shells amongst us, but they did us no injury, from the bank being covered with a bed of soft mud, in which they sank so deep, that in the explosion, nothing but clay was thrown up. When we got into a position, the French attempted to take it from us, in repulsing which Captain Dawson of the 52nd was killed. Being short of rations we were glad to pick up the acorns knocked down by the French bullets. During the night we had to bivouac on the ground which was flooded to the depth of several inches. We contrived to collect some stones into a heap, which enabled us to light a fire, but we actually lay in the water some inches deep during the night. On the 18th we continued the retreat, knee-deep in water. I have had many severe marches, but this was the worst I ever experienced. When we got to a rising ground, on which we were to bivouac, I fell completely exhausted. We arrived the next day at Rodrigo, and took up our winter quarters, after experiencing the heavy rains of spring at Badajos, and the heavy rains of autumn in the retreat. Few in this country can have any idea of their violence.

CHAPTER 4

St Sebastian

Having rested for five months, we started from Fuentes Guinalda on the 20th of May, 1813, to lead the advance of the main body of Lord Wellington's army. General Hill commanded the right wing, and General Graham the left. We passed the Douro on the 3rd of June, at the bridge of Toro, which had to be repaired for our passage, the French having previously blown it up. Lieutenant Pringle of the Engineers effected this by dropping ladders on each side, and laying planks from one to the other, a little above the water.

On the 12th of June, the Light Division, led by Grant's Hussars and Ponsonby's Dragoons, turned the French right, while the remainder of the troops attacked them in front, and turned their left, forcing them to retire. In retreating they blew up the Castle of Burgos, and by some mismanagement destroyed more than three hundred of their own men. Thus was effected without a shot on our part, that which had cost us so dearly to attempt in the last year's campaign. On the 13th we passed the Ebro.

Previous to our reaching the valley of the Ebro we had been marching over a plain to which there appeared to be no end, having no vegetation, when suddenly we found ourselves looking down into a beautiful valley, thickly planted with fruit trees, &c, and the river running in the centre; here we obtained many luxuries, of which we had been long deprived so far as our funds would allow, being several months pay in arrears; part of this advance we were obliged to cook with chopped straw, having no other fuel.

On the 18th of June we came across a French Brigade halting on the bank of a rivulet, waiting for a second brigade and their baggage. Both brigades were routed; the men threw away their knapsacks and made their escape, with the loss of at least three hundred prisoners and all their baggage. They then crossed the Zadora, where all the French armies were collecting to stop our progress.

On 21st the Light Division advanced to the neighbour-hood of the Zadora, and were halted on a height from which we had a full view of General Hill's movements on the ex-treme right, while Graham was turning the extreme left. General Hill attacked and drove the enemy from the heights occupied by their left wing. It was gallantly done, and was what Wellington was waiting for; to push forward the centre under his own immediate direction.

We were ordered to advance to the attack and under a heavy cannonade crossed one of the bridges over the Zadora. The seventh division having crossed another bridge on our left, our brigade was sent to reinforce them. We found them heavily raked by a French battery on their right. On this the 52nd, under Colonel Gibbs, advanced in column along the front of the height on which the guns were, and wheeling into line it was found necessary by an echelon movement to take up a new alignment. This was done with the same precision as it would be on a field-day, and a beautiful line was formed, the enemy's balls knocking a file out of it at every discharge; the Sergeants in rear calling out "Who got that?" and entering the names on their list, of casualties. The regiment then charged up the hill receiving a volley of grape without much loss, and driving the enemy before them over the plain on which Vittoria was situated. On this occasion our column of advance was at first in subdivisions, we were

70

left in front, and I had the command of one when a ball from the French battery passed over my head, and struck the third man on my left on the shoulder, taking his head off without doing more injury. He had only just joined us from home, and had said to his comrade the night before that he thought he would be killed in the expected battle. The cavalry presently came up, passed us, and took the pursuit. On reaching the city we found its neighbourhood covered with guns, baggage, stores of all descriptions, wagons full of money, carriages and conveyances of all kinds, with the immense concourse of Joseph's court. Of the siege trains and field batteries only two guns were carried off, one of which was disabled by a shot from our Horse Artillery, and taken on the 24th, as we continued the pursuit.

While passing through the centre of this immense body not a man was allowed to fall out, so that not an article was touched by us; stragglers and camp-followers were able to load themselves with it at their leisure. Indeed it may be said that the hard-working men of the Peninsular, generally speaking, got more kicks than halfpence. We were eighteen hours under arms on the 31st, having started at day-break, and followed the retreating enemy till darkness stopped their pursuit.

Clausel having on the 22nd of June (on his approach to Vittoria with fourteen thousand men) found the state of affairs, retired to Logrona, where he halted until the evening of the 25th, when Lord Wellington having got information of his movements sent the 5th and 6th Divisions after him, and proceeded with the 3rd, 4th and 7th, and the Light Division, with two brigades of Light Cavalry to intercept him, as he was making his way into France by Olite and Tafalla. We accomplished this by a long and weary night's march over the mountains, which lay between Pampeluna and these towns. Our division, after driving the only remaining gun which escaped from Vittoria into Pampeluna, left General Hill, with the 2nd division, to form its siege, and proceeded on the night march alluded to above. The part of the mountain we passed over would only admit of an advance in single file. Our general line of march was in sections of threes, which information was particularly suited to the Peninsular roads. The officer commanding the company rode at its head, the senior sub in the rear, the second with the captain in the front, and third sub with the first in the rear. For this purpose the companies were told off into threes, but instead of the old plans, the sections wheeled on its flank, and the command threes right, left, or front, was particularly adapted to the service, as well as the nature of the country. The state of the weather was similar to that of the night before the battle of Salamanca—there being torrents of rain, attended by tremendous peals of thunder and vivid flashes of lightning.

Having crossed the mountain, we were halted for the rear to close up, and I lay down with my horse's bridle over my arm. He had been a French troop horse, was taken at the battle of Fuentes d'Onor, and purchased from his captor by my brother. He would follow me about like a dog, and on this occasion, in the *war of elements,* remained by me while I slept. He would hold up his mouth to be kissed, and would stretch out his legs when ordered to do so, till his belly was nearly touching the ground, so that the rider could throw his leg over him without the use of the stirrup. Poor fellow, after seeing much hard service with his old masters, the French, and a good deal with ourselves, he lost his life in consequence of our being obliged to feed our horses on chopped furze; some of the spikes stuck in his tongue and could not be extracted, in consequence of which he was unable to eat and died from starvation.

During our passage over the mountain, Graham had driven Foy over the Bidassoa, and invested St. Sebastian, while Hill had driven Joseph and the remnant of his force into France, leaving the whole frontier of Spain, from the mouth of the Bidassoa to Roncesvalles, in our possession, with the exception of the two besieged cities. At this time Soult superseded Joseph, and took command of the French army, which, now re-organized and strongly reinforced with men and guns, oc-cupied the French frontier. Immediately in our front were the heights of Vera, which might more properly be called moun-tains than heights, and were almost perpendicular except on one point, which was strengthened with field-works and re-doubts, and might be considered impregnable. The position occupied by the Light Division was a much lower height running along the front.

On the 25th of July 1813, Soult, with sixty thousand men, forced the pass of Roncesvalles and Maya, and by a variety of skilful operations succeeded in his advance to the neighbour-hood of Pampeluna. Our troops were obliged to fall back (fighting), for reinforcements; the union of the 2nd Division, with the 3rd, 4th, 6th and 7th Divisions enabled them to check the enemy's advance in front, while the Light Division moved on his right flank.

General Graham, in the meantime, was obliged to sus-pend operations at St. Sebastian, and occupy the Bidassoa in force. Such was the state of affairs on the 29th of July, 1813. Soult had sent his wounded and artillery back to France, with orders to the latter to go round to the Lower Bidassoa, while he pushed across to St. Sebastian. In attempting this he was severely handled by Lord Wellington, and finding himself in a dilemma, the Light Division having headed him after most fatiguing marches and counter-marches amongst these lofty mountains, after which they returned to their old position at Vera.

The Bidassoa had a bend at Vera, from which it ran straight towards the sea for nine miles, after which it turned back to the rear on our left. There was a bridge over it, close to the town of Vera, in which we had a picquet. A few days before the final storming of St. Sebastian, fifty volunteers were called for from each regiment of the 3rd, 4th, and Light Divisions for this service. In the 52nd all were ready to do so, and the seniors were taken. A most gallant attack, which greatly contributed to our establishment in the town, was led by Captain Snodgrass of the 52nd, then serving as Major in the 13th Regiment of Portuguese Infantry, in Bradford's Brigade, which regiment he was in command of. Having ascertained that the inlet of the sea, which flowed under the walls, was fordable at low water, he volunteered to lead the 13th and 24th regiments through it to one of the breaches, which could not be attained in any other way. This was accomplished most gallantly under a murderous fire from the enemy,

While the storming of St. Sebastian was in progress, Soult having collected forty-five thousand men, crossed the Bidassoa by two pontoon bridges on the fords, on the 31st of August, between Vera and the sea, Clausel keeping the Light Division in check with a force at Vera. The latter also managed to establish himself on the other side of the bridge, and endeavoured with Gen. Reille to force their way to St. Sebastian. In this they failed, and were ordered by Soult to retreat; but unfortunately for Clausel, a heavy fall of rain had taken place, commencing at three o'clock which towards night rendered the fords impassable, and broke the pontoon bridges, rendering it impossible for his rear-guard to cross by any other means but the bridge at Vera, of which they managed to obtain possession during the storm which accompanied the rain. Fortunately, although we had been obliged to withdraw our picquet from Vera, there was a fortified house commanding the bridge, under the fire of which the enemy had to defile with fearful loss.

On the 1st September, Lord Beresford having placed a company of the 5th Portuguese Caçadores in Bradford's Brigade at Colonel Colborne's disposal, he gave me the appointment, and I proceeded at once to St. Sebastian to take command of it.

The company consisted of 120 men; one half were armed

with rifles, the other half with muskets and bayonets. On my arrival I found it under the fire of the Castle, which still held out, but finally surrendered on the 3rd of September.

The fall of St. Sebastian having enabled Lord Wellington to take the offensive, he took the bold step of crossing the Bidassoa, and establishing his left in the strong position occupied by the French right. This was effected in the following manner:—Soult was led to think that the attack would come from the right of our army at Roncesvalles, where there was no obstacle, instead of from the left, where there was a river only passable at low water. Being under this impression; he allowed his troops to be engaged in the construction of field works, at some distance from the mouth of the river. While they were thus engaged Lord Wellington got up his pontoons, and in the night of the 6th of October, in the midst of a violent thunderstorm, collected his troops close to the fords at the mouth of the river.

On the 7th, everything answering, the tents were left standing to deceive the enemy, and as soon as day broke, our columns moved forward across the fords, driving the enemy before them. At the same time the Light Division, with a division of Spaniards, made their attack on the French position at Vera, and on the mountain between it and the mouth of the river. In this attack the 52nd bore a prominent part under Colonel Colborne, who commanded the brigade. As I was engaged at the mouth of the river with Bradford's Brigade, I can only say, that having been in position opposite the pass at Vera, from the latter end of June to the 1st September, 1813, I was eye-witness to the field works and redoubts, one above the other, daily erecting by the French, and if any one had told me that it would have been carried as it was, I would have said it was impossible.

CHAPTER 5

Into France

At the battle of the Nivelle the French position extended from the source of the Nivelle to its mouth at St. Jean de Luz; the centre, commanded by Clausel occupied a range of hills on our side of the river, which swept round them from flank to flank. The whole of their position was entrenched and covered with field works, in which the French were busily occupied from the 7th October to the 10th November, the day of the battle. On this occasion the Light Division was engaged with Clausel's right, and succeeded in forcing him from his position. The 52nd bore a very active part, of which I was witness from Bradford's Brigade, which was moved from the coast to the support of their Brigade. Their charge up the hill to attack their entrenchments was very fine. Being sent by General Bradford with an order to the rear, after the action, I was for the first time a witness of camp-followers rifling the dead, and was in some danger from interfering without support.

By this action the way was opened for our advance on Bayonne. My brigade returned to the left wing, now under the command of General Hope, under whom we advanced to Bidart and its neighbourhood.

After the battle of Nivelle, Lord Wellington, from the state of the roads, gave us a month's rest in cantonments; the enemy occupying his entrenched camp in front of Bayonne, from the

Adour above the town, to the Adour below the town, which communicated by means of bridges, and having advanced posts extending on the right bank of the Nive to Cambo, where he had a large force.

This was done with equal gallantry, but with great exertion from the state of the roads, which were knee-deep with mud. Our force was twenty-four thousand men, and the Royal road from Bayonne to St. Jean de Luz was better than the cross roads. The Ninth Regiment, led by my company of Caçadores as an advanced guard, were in front. After passing the Mayor of Biarritz's house, I came in contact with the enemy, who occupied a height on the right of the road, and commenced skirmishing with them. This led to a disagreement with the gallant commander of the Ninth who mistook them for Spaniards, and wanted me to cease firing; however, a few minutes convinced him of his error, as several of our men were killed and wounded while we were talking. The enemy soon found it necessary to retire to his entrenched camp, within gunshot of which I occupied a house, and held it till evening. General Bradford's orders were to get my company into fire wherever I could. Acting on this order, by advancing in double time, I got to the head of the column on the Royal road—the Ninth Regiment was the leading regiment of the 5th Division. Gleig, in his *Subaltern*, makes the following allusions to this skirmish:

> The night of the 8th passed quietly over, and I arose about two hours before dawn on the 9th, perfectly fresh and, like those around me, in high spirits. We had been so long idle, that the near prospect of a little fighting, instead of creating gloomy sensations, was viewed with sincere delight; and we took our places, and began our march towards the high-road, in silence, it is true, but with extreme good will. There we remained stationary till the day broke, when, the word being given to advance, we rushed forward in the direction of Bayonne.

The brigade to which I belonged took post at the head of the 1st Division, and immediately in the rear of the 6th. This situation afforded to me, on several occasions, as the inequalities placed me, from time to time, on the summit of an eminence, very favourable opportunities of behold-ing the whole of the warlike mass which was moving; nor is it easy to imagine a more imposing or more elevating spectacle. The entire left wing of the army advanced, in a single continuous column, by the main road, and cov-ered, at the most moderate computation, a space of four miles. As far, indeed, as the eye could reach, nothing was to be seen except swarms of infantry, clothed not only in scarlet, but in green, blue, and brown uniforms; whilst here and there a brigade of four or six guns occupied a vacant space between the last files of one division and the first of another. In rear of all came the cavalry, but of their appearance I was unable accurately to judge, they were so far distant.

We had proceeded about five miles, and it was now sev-en o'clock, when, our advanced guard falling in with the French picquets, a smart skirmish began. It was really a beautiful sight. The enemy made, it is true, no very de-termined stand, but they gave not up a rood of ground, without exchanging a few shots with their assailants, who pressed forward, vigorously indeed, but with all the cau-tion and circumspection which mark the advance of a skilful skirmisher. The column, in the meanwhile, moved slowly but steadily on, nor was it once called upon, during, the whole of the day, to deploy into line.

In the evening we retired to our cantonments, leaving our outposts at the Mayor's house, the Light Division being on its right, with a body of French in their front. Dur-ing the night of the 9th December, Soult collected sixty thousand men in the entrenched camp on the left bank of the Nive; with this force he advanced at daybreak on the morning of the 10th, attacking Campbell's Portuguese Brigade, who occupied the plantations round the Mayor's house. This post was maintained singly by the latter till our Brigade (which was about two miles in the rear) came to their assistance, the enemy gradually working their way through the wood on our right flank; we had frequently to retire until they were driven back. On one of these occasions I was running on one side of the hedge, and the French on the other, when my cap fell off—I was doubtful of having time to pick it up, but putting down my hand I got hold of it. On getting to the end of the hedge, I found our supports coming up, when we returned the compliment, and the enemy had to run back as fast as they had run forward.

In the same book Gleig goes on to describe this scene:

And now the scene of action began to open upon us. We had passed through Bidart, and were descending on the little eminence on which it was built, when the combatants became distinguishable: and a very magnificent as well as gratifying spectacle they presented. The merest handful of British troops were opposing themselves, in the most determined manner, to a mass of men so dense and so extended as to cover the whole of the main road so far as the eye could reach. Our people were, it is true, giving way; they had already maintained a most unequal contest of upwards of two hours, and their numbers, originally small, were fast diminishing. But no sooner had the head of our column shown itself than their confidence completely returned, and renewed the struggle with increased alacrity. For being able to drive them back we were indebted to the gallantry of the 9th Regiment under Colonel Cameron.

My appearance at this time was not very elegant. I had on a pair of white trousers (or rather a pair of trousers that had been white). I also wore a pair of new worsted gloves, the blue of which came off most freely on the trousers, after the heavy showers which we were exposed to, and rendered their appearance ridiculous, and as I was a most conspicuous figure, rallying my men, after getting out of the wood, I almost wonder Gleig did not remark it. I have been told that my Lieut.-Colonel St. Clair, who was fond of drawing, drew the scene, introducing me into it, but I did not hear that he introduced the whitey-blue trousers.

The fighting continued till dark, when I was ordered to place a chain of communication between the troops on our right and those on our left; in doing this I was obliged to reconnoitre the ground and the position of the enemy, in doing which I was very nearly captured; on my way along our front I could perceive some dark figures on a rising ground in front of a house. Leaving a few men I had with me, at some distance, I advanced and challenged them; the answer was in Portuguese, so I called on one of them to advance, and the answer was, "Come here, you," the Spanish word for 'you' being used instead of the Portuguese word, which satisfied me that it was the enemy I had to deal with. In posting my chain of sentries, we had melancholy evidence of the severity of the action in the number of bodies we had stumbled over; this was the case all through the plantation. Out of 11 officers brought into action, the 5th Caçadores had eight killed and wounded! The proceedings of the Light Division on our right will be found in Napier, vol. 6. On going to General Bradford's quarters in the Mayor's house, I found him with General Hay and a number of field officers; on reporting that I had completed our chain of communication, I had the satisfaction of receiving their thanks for my services on the last two days.

It appears from the above facts that my company of the 5th Caçadores commenced the battles of the Nive, but so little do men know of what is going on around them when engaged, that I was not aware of it until putting my recollections together for this little work.

At daybreak on the morning of the 11th, being on the look out for the enemy, I found they had withdrawn from the posts occupied during the night, which I immediately reported to General Bradford, who ordered me to move forward and ascertain what they were about—the General riding with us on a large white horse. We came upon the enemy in great force, who had hidden themselves behind the tank in our front. I at once told General Bradford that they would pick him off, but he continued to expose himself till his horse was shot under him.

By his order I attacked a breastwork in our front, and drove the enemy from it. While doing so I received a blow in the breast from a spent ball. Several of my men heard it strike me, and they called out "The Captain is killed!" in a tone of surprise and sorrow—they appeared to think me invulnerable. I take this opportunity of stating that the soldiers of my company became greatly attached to me, and when I was leaving, after being wounded in the sortie from Bayonne, they actually cried like children. It may appear singular that I should receive such a blow from the spent ball without being wounded, but having the breast of my jacket thickly braided with silk cord, and a silk handkerchief in my breast, the resistance offered by the silk saved me.

The French advancing in force on our right, we were obliged to re-occupy the ridge in front of the Mayor's house, which was attacked in various parts and with various successes till evening, when we still held our ground. The 12th passed off with a heavy cannonade from both sides, which caused considerable havoc.

On the 13th, Soult leaving three Divisions in the entrenched camp in our front, moved the rest of his army to the right bank of the Nive, and attacked Hill, who was placed at great disadvantage. The heavy rain on the 12th had caused his bridge to be carried away, and it took some time to restore it, but he held his ground and finally triumphed. These five days' fighting in which the enemy suffered severely, caused him to retreat behind the Adour, and finally from his entrenched camp at Bayonne.

We re-occupied our cantonments after the battles of the Nive, and had nearly two months' rest before we were again actively employed. On the 23rd February, 1814, Bradford's Brigade having been brought to the front, I was sent with my company to occupy an advanced post close to the entrenched camp at Biarritz, and having posted my sentries within a short distance of the enemy's, without opposition, we made ourselves as comfortable as circumstances would permit. Shortly after I was ordered to drive in the enemy, and occupy their post. As they had allowed me to post my sentries close to theirs, I considered myself bound in honour not to take advantage of them. I therefore visited mine, and told them to fall back as soon as I should wave my cap; and having returned to my post, I ordered the company to fall in, and stepping forward waved my cap to the enemy's sentries, who took the hint and retired to their main body, while mine did the same. We then advanced and continued skirmishing till evening, when we retired to our former post. We were relieved by a detachment of Spaniards, and were moved towards the sea and the entrance of the Adour. Here we were witness on the 24th of February to the gallant passage of our gunboats and sailing vessels, prepared by Lord Wellington to form a bridge over the river. The passage was most difficult, there being a heavy surf and a bar at the mouth of the river, which was only passable in one narrow spot. After passing it, the river suddenly turned to the left, and if a vessel lost her way she was driven on shore. This occurred in several instances, and there were several boats and vessels upset in the passage, and all the crews drowned, with the exception of one midshipman, who was picked up by a gunboat. Unfortunately he was only saved from one death to undergo another—the gunboat was driven on shore, and fell on her side—he was thrown out upon the sand, when the gun fell upon his body and killed him. During the night of the 23rd and morning of the 24th Colonel Stopford and six hundred of the Guards passed the river (eight hundred yards wide and very rapid, running seven miles an hour at ebb tide) in a raft made of two pontoons; the rocket battery also passed, which, with the field battery on our side, repulsed an attack from the garrison of Bayonne. In the evening the remainder of the 1st Division and our Brigade crossed on the raft and protected the parties forming the bridge, which was three miles below Bayonne. This bridge was completed on the 25th. The first Division and Bradford's Brigade, numbering eight thousand men, invested the fortress from the Adour above to the Adour below, the distance being about two miles; the Spaniards invested the two parts of the entrenched camp on the other side of the Adour. The garrison was said to consist of fifteen thousand picked men. On the 27th of February we drove the enemy into the fortress, contracting our investment to half-pistol shot in the centre, which was opposite the citadel, and everything was prepared for a siege. With the exception of a shot from the fortress, (when they could get an object to fire at), nothing particular occurred till the 14th of April, when the enemy made a sortie on our advanced posts at St. Etienne, and succeeded in forcing their way through our troops, killed General Hay, and taking General Hope and Colonel Townsend prisoners. General Hay's wife and daughters had joined him from England a few days before the sortie. General Hinaber with his Germans succeeded in stopping the enemy; in this engagement the 5th Caçadores took an active part.

We occupied a gentleman's country house in rear of the outposts, and having heard the night before of the peace having been concluded at Paris, the Governor of Bayonne having likewise been informed of it, we retired to rest under the impression that the last shot had been fired—what was our astonishment to be awakened a little before daylight by the enemy's balls flying through our windows. A few minutes found us under arms, and on the left of the Germans, with whom we advanced to the relief of the troops engaged, driving the French into their fortress. Being in command of a wing of the Caçadores, I had them in column in front of the citadel, waiting to see if any further attack would take place, when a ball from the walls wounded one of my men, on which I moved the column behind a house on my left, remaining myself on the look out. Suddenly I felt a blow on the shin, and on looking down found that a ball had entered between the two bones, carrying in a piece of the trousers, which I believe was the last shot fired.

On returning to my quarters I found it occupied as an hospital. General Hay lay dead in the room I had slept in, and General Bradford was under the hands of a surgeon. On seeing me General Bradford ordered the surgeon to stop, and attend to my wound before he finished his dressing.

After writing the above, the manuscript being in the printer's hands, the following article appeared in the *United Service Magazine* for June, 1859, being part of the *Reminiscences of a Veteran*:

> I was now perfectly recovered, when an order arrived for me to do duty, and take command of the 6th Caçadores in the 2nd Division; so taking leave of my former comrades, I proceeded on my journey. I had a short time before received the arrears of my pay as Major of Brigade, so I had plenty of money. I also escaped from the sortie the garrison made afterwards, and I can conceive from their proximity that the Caçadores must have been roughly handled. Poor Dobbs, after boasting that he had remained uninjured the whole of the war, received on this occasion a wound in the heel, which laid him up for several months.

On seeing this extract, I wrote the editor of the *United Service Magazine* a letter showing that my friend Bunbury was mistaken as to my wound being in the heel, and explaining the part taken by the Caçadores in this affair.

I was sent into quarters in the neighbourhood for the recovery of my wound; the natives showed me as much attention as if I had been their own countryman. After some time I was sent to St. Jean de Luz, where I met with the same kindness. I then embarked for Oporto, where I remained for some time, being billeted on a Portuguese merchant, from whom also I received great kindness. I required this, being actually penniless, although I had six month's pay due to me.

The cause of my being without money was the difficulties raised by their pay office, although I had brought all necessary certificates from the regiment. They are still in my debt the Peninsular prize-money, although trifling, and I have long ceased to look for it. I only got my pay a few days before starting. While at Oporto I was invited to a feast; it was a very disgusting scene, There was a great number of dishes, and almost all the guests made it a point to eat of every dish, and when too full, would go out and get rid of what they had eaten and return to begin afresh, while there was Britons at this time, who acted in the same way with drink. We must give the Portuguese credit for sobriety, except in expectation of a fight, when they would take a pull at their ration rum, and they were surprised when I would not take a *share*, telling them that we would do better without it. The officer made no bones in confessing that they had no relish for fighting, and would tell me "You English love fighting!"

I said "No, but when duty calls we go".

A custom amongst the Portuguese females was that of rouging while young, they are very well-looking, but when they begin to lose their colour, they commence this foolish habit, which turns them nearly black, except when daubed over with paint.

Being then withdrawn from the Portuguese service by the British Government, I embarked for Dublin in a merchant vessel. In laying in my sea-stock I got a mall cask of port wine which was prepared for the English market, and which, I expected would be such as was in use at home, but I found it anything but palatable being half brandy.

On embarking, I had to leave my Caçadore servant behind me, and I cannot help feeling excited whilst I write when I remember his frantic despair at our separation; he was a reserved silent man, which made it more remarkable. As we sailed up the Irish Channel, our vessel struck on a rock off the coast of Wicklow, and I landed, and in doing so, one of my crutches broke, and I had to hop over a sandy beach for some distance, whereby I received an injury in the other leg, from which I still suffer. I succeeded in getting a seat in a stage coach to Dublin, and arrived there to the surprise of my friends, who had an evening party. I was rather an uncommon figure for Dublin, my Portuguese uniform and long beard being a new thing there.

I was suffering under my wound for a year, during which time I was promoted to a company in the 52nd, and on Buonaparte escaping from Elba, I found myself able to throw away my crutches, and left Dublin to join the 2nd Battalion of the 52nd, then in Belgium with Lord Wellington, as was also the 1st Battalion.

On reporting myself at the Horse Guards, I received orders to take command of the depot of the 2nd Battalion at Dover, and shortly after joined the skeleton of the Battalion at Canterbury. The effective men of this Battalion had been drafted into the 1st Battalion, which bore a prominent part in the crisis of the battle of Waterloo.

The following description of this crisis, extracted from *Siborne*, vol. 2, will serve to give an idea of the nature of the combat at the time when the French were finally forced to give way:

> Had the second column of attack continued in the original direction of its advance, it would have come upon the centre of Adam's Brigade, but having, as it began to ascend the exterior slope of the main ridge of the allied position, slightly diverged to its right, as before observed, by following the direction of a very gentle hollow, con-

stituting the re-entering angle, formed by the tongue of ground that projected from the front of Maitland's Brigade, and that part of the ridge occupied by Adam's Brigade, it, in some degree, bent its flank to the latter. This circumstance was not only observed, but had been in a great measure anticipated by Lieutenant Colonel Sir John Colborne, commanding the 52nd Regiment, an officer of great repute in the British army. He had been watching with intense anxiety, the progress of the enemy's column, and, seizing the most favourable moment, he, without orders, and upon his own responsibility, wheeled the left company of the 52nd, and then formed the remainder of the regiment upon that company, for the purpose of bringing its front nearly parallel with the flank of the French column. At this moment Adam rode up and asked Colborne what he was going to do, to which the latter replied, 'To make that column feel our fire.' Adair, approving of this, ordered Colborne to move on, and galloped off to bring up his right regiment, the 71st. The Duke, who had just seen Maitland's Brigade re-formed and posted in the best order, parallel with the front of the attacking column, was at this moment stationed on the right of Napier's battery. He despatched an *aide-de-camp* (Major the Hon. Henry Percy) to direct Sir Henry Clinton to advance and attack the Imperial Guard; but a single glance at Colborne's forward movement satisfied him that his intention was anticipated; and he immediately pushed forward the 2nd Battalion, 95th Regiment, to the left of the 52nd. The head of the French column had by this time nearly readied the brow of the ridge, its front covering almost the whole of Napier's battery, and a portion of the extreme fight of Maitland's Brigade. It was still gallantly pressing forward, in defiance of the most galling fire poured into its front by the battery and by the British Guards, when the sudden and imposing appearance of the four-deep line of the 52nd Regiment, bearing directly towards its left flank, in the most admirable and compact order imaginable, caused it to halt. In the next instant, wheeling up its left sections, it opened a rapid and destructive lire from the entire length of its flank against the 52nd Regiment. Colborne, having brought his line parallel to the flank of the Imperial Guard, also halted, and poured a deadly fire into the mass; and almost at the same moment the rifles of the 2nd Battalion, 95th Regiment, then coming up on the left were levelled and discharged with unerring aim into the more advanced portion of the column. The 71st Regiment was at this time rapidly advancing on the right to complete the Brigade movement. Colborne, eagerfully to carry out his projected flank attack upon the enemy's column caused his men to cease firing, and then gave the command, 'Charge! Charge!' It was answered by three hearty British cheers that rose distinctly above the shouts of 'Vive l'Empereur!' and the now straggling and unsteady fire from the column. The 2nd Battalion, 95th Regiment, hastened to join in the charge on the left. The movement was remarkable for the order, the steadiness, the resolution, and the daring by which it was characterized. The column of the Imperial Guard, which already seemed to reel to and fro under the effect of the front and flank fire, which had been so successfully brought to bear upon it, was evidently in consternation as it beheld the close advance of Adam's Brigade. Some daring spirits—and it contained many within its ranks— still endeavoured to make at least a show of resistance; but the disorder, which had been rapidly increasing, now became uncontrollable; and the second column of the Imperial Guard breaking into the wildest confusion, shared the fate of the first, with this difference, however, that in consequence of the combined front and flank fire in which it had been so fatally involved, and of the unrestrained pursuit which deprived it of the power of rallying its component parts, it became so thoroughly disjointed and dispersed, that with the exception of the two rear battalions, which constituted the 1st Regiment of chasseurs (Old Guard), it is extremely doubtful whether any portion of it ever re-united as a regularly formed military body during the brief remaining period of the battle—certainly not on the allied side of La Belle Alliance, towards which point it directed its retreat. It is necessary to remark that this regiment of the Old Guard, which was commanded by General Cambronne, formed a separate column of support in echelon to, and immediately in the left rear of, the four battalions of the Middle Guard; but so close to each other were the two columns that although an interval was observed between them by Adam's Brigade, when the latter stood in the general front line of the allied position, they appeared to it as but one column when charged in flank, and may, to all intents and purposes, be considered as hating formed one general column of attack; Cambronne's battalions, however, forming the rear of the column, did not become exposed to the fire from Adam's Brigade, inasmuch as neither the 71st Regiment, nor the 3rd Battalion, 95th Regiment, could complete the Brigade flank movement in time to open a fire upon the mass before the actual charge was commenced. Hence, although they turned, along with the rest of the column, yet, unlike the latter, they retained a considerable degree of order."[1]

The direction to Adam's line, by its right shoulder forward movement having brought it perpendicular to the general front of the French position, that officer became naturally anxious for support upon his right flank, to secure the latter from the enemy's cavalry, which, it was to be presumed, would now be brought forward from his reserve. Since none of it had been employed in immediate support of the last attack.

He urgently requested for this purpose the aid of troops

---

1. In Siborne's 1st volume, pages 376-7, it will be seen that the British had only 24,000 men and 76 guns, at Waterloo, while the French had 72,000 men, and 246 guns; most of the British allies were worse than useless.

from the other part of Clinton's division, and Lieut.-Colonel Halkett, seeing what was required, immediately advanced with the nearest battalion of his Hanoverian Brigade, the Osnabruck band were in column at quarter distance, and close up in right rear of the 71st Regiment. Thus, Adam's Brigade, maintaining its four deep line, and being flanked by the Hanoverian battalion, which could form squares at any moment, was sufficiently secured against the cavalry.

The confused and disordered mass of the Imperial Guard from the first impulse given it by the flank charge, hastened a short distance in a direction parallel with that or the Anglo-allied line, and then naturally inclining towards the French position, it fell into nearly the same track as that pursued by the first attacking column, *viz.*, towards the first rise of ground intersected by the Charleroi road, a little beyond the Southern extremity of the Orchard of La Haye Saint.

As it approaches the rear of those columns d'Erlon's Corps, which had been so desperately opposing Alton's division, it became infected with the panic, and co-mingled with the flying guard, Adam's Brigade continued its triumphant advance, at first parallel, for a short distance to the allied line, and then, bringing forward its left shoulders, swept proudly forward in the direction of the French height before mentioned, crowds of fugitives hurrying along, and striving to escape from the pursuing wave that seemed every instant on the point of engulfing them.

During its advance, the front of Adam's Brigade was partially crossed by the squadron of the 23rd Light Dragoons, who was unfortunately fired upon by the 52nd regiment, and it was not until the foremost of them had fallen close upon the bayonets that the error was discovered. Immediately after this incident, a fire of grape was opened upon the 52nd by three French field pieces in the prolongation of its right flank. This enfilading of the regiment, in its four-deep line, was a judicious measure on the part of the French artillery, and well calculated to derange the advance of Adam's Brigade. It was, however, very gallantly and speedily checked by the wheeling up and advance of the right section of the 52nd, under Lieutenant Gawber, who succeeded in driving off the guns whilst the rest of the regiment continued the pursuit.

Wellington, as soon as he saw that the success of the charge by Adam's Brigade was so decisive, requested Uxbridge immediately to launch forward some fresh cavalry the probable advance of that of the enemy, and to second the efforts of the infantry in front, by boldly attacking the French reserves which appeared collected in front of La Belle Alliance, the critical point of Napoleon's line. Lieut.-Colonel Lord Greenock, Quarter-Master-General of the cavalry, was dispatched to Vivian, with orders for him to move his hussar brigade to its right from its position in rear of Alton's division, so as to get clear of their infantry, and then advance directly to the front by the right of Maitland's Brigade of guards. At the same time the Duke turned round to order up the nearest supports to the space which had been vacated in his front line by the advance of Adam's Brigade. But what a spectacle met his view. The three Dutch Belgium squares into which d'Aubrene's Brigade had been formed, and whose unsteadiness, previously described, had greatly augmented as the firing and shouting on the exterior slope of the ridge, of which they could see nothing, became more continuous and intense, were now in a state bordering on dissolution. The faces of the squares were already broken at intervals by groups in the act of abandoning their ranks; whilst several officers of Vandeleur's Brigade, which, as before observed, was drawn up in their rear were zealously exerting themselves to induce these troops to stand fast. The Duke, observing this, called out, "That's right; tell them the French are retiring." This intelligence quickly caught up and spread through their ranks, had the desired effect of restoring them to order. They shortly afterwards formed in columns, and advanced to the front line.

Battle of Waterloo, deducting loss at Quatre-Bras[1]

Effective strength of British, 18th June	21,026
Effective strength of Germans	21,851
Total	49,877

Belgians occupied some of these troops,
keeping them in their ranks

Loss of British, in killed, wounded and missing	6,064
Loss of Germans, in killed, wounded and missing	1,381

The brunt fell on the British, their loss per cent
was 28·8. Loss of Germans was only 4·7.

I calculate that at this crisis, we had not more than 12,000 effective British, after deducting killed, wounded, and men occupied with the wounded.

It may be satisfactory to compare our circumstances after the battle of Waterloo with the state of affairs in 1798. At that time Ireland had four hundred thousand inhabitants in open rebellion, and had actually been invaded by a French force; not very large, it is true, but still able to advance unmolested into the interior. Their conquests on the continent were rapidly progressing; they had a powerful fleet and army under the direction of Bonaparte, a man of first-rate talents, with all the continent under his control. Against these powers England had to contend single-handed for the greater portion of the time till in 1816, the French fleet had ceased to exist, Bonaparte had been hurled from his dominions, and Great Britain was at peace with all the continental powers, and continued so till the Crimean war, a period of thirty-eight years.

---

1. *Siborne*, vol. 2.

Chapter 6

Home Again

After the battle of Waterloo, the 2nd Battalion was reduced, and as I was junior captain. I lost all hopes of active employment. On this I married one of my next door neighbours, whom I had left a child, but found on my return from the Peninsula, a fine young woman. On the evening of my return, we met at my mother's as strangers; she not having been told of my arrival, and I never supposing her to be the child I had left six years before.

On my reduction I returned to Dublin, via Liverpool, and experienced the disadvantage of travelling in these days. After a tedious journey of two days and a night on the top of a coach, I went to a hotel till a packet should be ready to sail; but having become acquainted with a mercantile traveller on the coach, he told me that I might be detained for a week or more, and that my best plan was to take lodgings. I followed his advice and we remained together for a fortnight before I could get a passage, and when we did sail, we only got as far as the Hill of Howth, when we encountered a violent gale, which drove us back to Holyhead, where we were obliged to remain for several days. All my money being spent before I left Liverpool, I was obliged to borrow what I required to bring me over.

Up to this period I was in utter ignorance of my state before God, and the ground of a sinner's hope. The state of the

Protestants was lamentable; there was only one clergyman of the Established Church preaching the Gospel in Dublin, and he was silenced as far as the bishop was able. His appointment was from the trustees of the Bethesda; he was not allowed into any other pulpit, nor was any other clergyman allowed into his. The abuse which was lavished upon him by the old card-players and ball-goers led me to respect him, and I occasionally went to hear him; and although his sermons were an hour long, yet they were so well connected that I was never tired of them. The state of society was very bad—drinking, swearing, gambling, duelling, &c, &c, were almost universal.

During a visit to the North of Ireland, I was taken ill at Carrickfergus, where my sister's family was, and while confined to my room, took a book from a shelf to read; the process of vegetation, as described in it, led me to think of the Great Being who had made all things. About this time a lady directed me to justification by faith in the merits of the Redeemer, and not by our own works ; against this I fought hard.

About this time the Irish Evangelical Society sent a minister to Carrickfergus, and the violent abuse with which he was assailed awakened my curiosity to hear what he had to say, which I found to agree with the Apostolic doctrine. He preached Jesus and the Resurrection—holding Him up as a Prince and a Saviour, exalted to the right hand of God, to give repentance and forgiveness of sins to his people. I became a constant attendant; after some time the duty of *breaking bread,* was brought under our notice, which caused me to examine the nature of the Apostolic churches, and led me to unite with the brethren who had thus been brought together in fellowship and breaking of bread. This gave great offence to all my friends, and caused a good deal of ridicule as far as it could be exercised.

On Mr. Flintons first going to Carrickfergus he obtained the use of the Assembly-rooms for preaching in. For some time it was crowded, but there was a general outcry against him from the clergymen of all denominations, and it was taken from him and he was obliged to remove to what was called the old Court-house. This was when I first attended his ministry. In wet weather the rain came in in all directions, still it was considered a great favour to get it, which, if I recollect right, was granted by my cousin, the Rev. R. Dobbs, and who was, at that time, mayor. Under these circumstances it was proposed to build a place of worship; and Mr. Ellis, a gentleman of property in the neighbourhood; gave a site near the castle together with a handsome subscription. This aroused the enemies to perfect rage, and an attempt was made to stop it by claiming the ground as lying waste for the public use.

The attempt failed and the building was commenced under threats of being pulled down as fast as it was built. At last it was roofed in, but whether any foul play had taken place or the foundation was bad, one of the walls gave way, and there was a great shout of joy from those who wished it down, while the friends of its erection were nearly in despair; it was, however, finished and occupied. The little church formed, and bread was broken in it.

About this time the 43rd Regiment was quartered in Belfast, and our Captain Maddens, brother, was detached to Carrickfergus. It was he who was supposed to be mortally wounded in the ditch at Badajos. When his brother was killed, it was he who sought a copy of the Scriptures but could not get it. While dining with him at a clergyman's house in Carrickfergus, I heard so much ridicule of Mr. Flinton and his congregation that I got up and left the room—this led Madden to attend our meeting. After he had recovered from his wound at Badajos he relapsed into his former careless state, but just before his visit to Carrickfergus he had attended the death of a favourite brother of the 95th Regiment at Liverpool, which was the means of awakening him permanently, and he has since become a clergyman in the establishment.

My old prisoner, Major O'Kelly, also was detached to Carrickfergus from Belfast, and a few years since having paid a visit to my friends in the North, I was with my brother-in-law at Cusnendall and strolled into a tower where they kept prisoners, when in conversation with the keeper—an old pensioner—I asked him what regiment he belonged to? His answer was the 11th, on which I asked him if he knew Major O'Kelly? His reply was that he was his servant, and was often with him on his reconnoitring parties, but on the occasion I met Major O'Kelly it was unsafe to take him with him.

I have now the happiness of finding almost all the members of my family taking more or less active parts in the cause of truth, some in India, others in America, and many at home. It has also been a privilege to have my simple testimony to the Saviour bearing fruit, of which I was not aware for years after the seed was sown.

Having returned to Dublin, I was shortly after married, and went to reside in Carrickfergus, where I remained till 1823, when the Duke of Wellington having been appointed Master-General of the Ordnance, gave me the Barrack-mastership of Nenagh, in the county of Tipperary. Before leaving Carrickfergus I had seen every house supplied with the scriptures, and left a school under the Kildare Street Society at full work. This barrack district comprised some of the worst parts of Galway, Clare, Limerick, and Tipperary. Whilst on this service, I was privileged to give my assistance to the London Hibernian School Society, the Evangelical, Bible, and some other Societies, having the same objects in view, by which some thousand copies of the Scriptures passed through my hands. On one occasion a lady in the neighbourhood sent me an enquiring Roman Catholic who had got possession of a Bible. In conversation I happened to show him the nature of the primitive churches, and the fellowship that should exist among its members. He said "I have been looking for that for some time, and I'll join you."

Accordingly Doctor Townley, the Independent minister

of Limerick, (whose private income carried on the work he was engaged in) having come over to Nenagh, Daniel Moran, Miss Molloy and myself broke bread with him, in a cabin which I had fitted up as a place of worship. This beginning resulted in a number of converts from the Church of Rome, and an awakening among the Protestants, and the formation of small churches of a similar nature at Castletown, Borris-o-Kane, and at Leap Castle, which afterwards was the origin of what are now called the Plymouth Brethren. The revivals in the North of Ireland at the present moment, 1859, have drawn to my recollection a remarkable instance of the deep conviction which a Protestant friend of mine underwent; he laboured for some time under similar depression, but when he saw clearly the remedy in the Gospel, met with similar relief; he was brother to one of the first members of our little church, but shortly after died rejoicing in the Saviour. These Christian brethren have been scattered abroad, but I have been occasionally gratified by hearing of their steadfastness in the Faith; I have also found that the Scriptures which passed through my hands have been treasured by many who did not dare to make an open profession.

The following instance of the effect produced by reading the Scriptures gave me great satisfaction:

Having taken shelter in a cabin one day from a heavy shower of rain, I found an old man sitting by the fire, as usual, he offered me a seat and I sat down, and we got into chat, first on general subjects, and afterwards on Scriptural truths, with which he was greatly interested, on which I asked him if he would like to have a Testament, he said he would, so I sent him one by Daniel Moran, he kept it for about two month's, and was reading it almost day and night, at which his friends became greatly alarmed and called in the priest, who wanted him to burn it, he said he would do no such thing, but for peace-sake he would return it to the gentleman who gave it to him, he accordingly gave it to Moran, who generally passed his door on his way to Nenagh, to bring it back to me, telling Moran his reasons. Some time after doing so, being in a dying state he requested his. neighbour, Mr. Dungan of Nigh, to assist him in making his will, which led to a conversation on his hopes of salvation, which he declared to be on the Saviour, to the exclusion of all creatures. On Mr. Dungan asking him how he came to this conclusion, he said, by reading a Testament given him by a gentleman, but, said Mr. Dungan, Captain Dobbs told me you only kept it a short time. "Short time as it was said he, I found there was only one Saviour in it."

About the time that the above circumstance occurred I happened to visit my friends in Dublin, and heard that a Christian friend and neighbour was in the last stage of water on the chest. Every year she had been in the habit of sending me a little, Christian remembrance, but I had no idea that there was anything more meant by it. On this occasion she expressed a wish to see me, and I found her gasping for breath. She said, "John, you were the first to speak to me of Jesus."

The Ordnance Department, particularly the Barrack Department, was full of abuses when it came into the hands of the Duke, from which, when I left in 1841, it was almost clear.

One article of barrack accommodation compared with the present period, will give an idea of the difference. Most of the barracks were houses hired for the purpose, having a number of low, small rooms. The permanent barracks had larger ones, but all were filled with double wooden bedsteads, touching each other, which contained four men, two above and two below, and the crevices of the wood were full of bugs.

One instance will show the system of abuse which prevailed up to the Duke's time. Coals were kept in large open yards, and issued by measure, and the barrack-master was allowed to charge a certain proportion for waste. The fact was, however, that a large surplus arose from the slaking of the coals. Under the new system the public get credit for every pound surplus, so that the saving is very great indeed.

My district at Nenagh was a lawless one, and at times my visits to out-stations, which were numerous, were frequently attended with personal danger; daily murders were committed, and in the year 1825 Pastorini's prophecy was expected to be fulfilled by a universal massacre of Protestants, and immense collections of people marched through the country, with green sashes, and banners flying, moving in perfect order, in sections, with a large body of mounted men, acting as cavalry. While preparing my little place of worship, they marched past it, Daniel Moran, who was a mason by trade, being at the time engaged in the work, but his faith was strong, and he remained unmoved. Previous to his conversion Moran was the leader of a large faction which had regular pitched battles at Borris-o-Kane. On one occasion, his party being inferior in number to his adversaries, he made them take off their coats, saying that it would prevent any one going away—his party gained the victory. He manifested the same boldness in his Christian course by bearing the reproaches and attacks of his friends and neighbours, many of whom afterwards adopted his views; he had four brothers and one sister who with their families joined him and his family; the children were as bold as their parents.

In visiting one of my out-stations—Tomgrany—at the other side of the Shannon and in the County Galway I had an opportunity of seeing the dreadful consequences of the old tithe system. There being no inn in the village, I was requested by the clergyman to take a bed at his Glebe, which was a short distance from the village. After visiting the barrack I believe I dined with the officer in command, and at dusk proceeded to my night quarters. On arriving at the hall-door and tapping I heard dogs barking and a great bustle inside from whence I was challenged, and on giving a satisfactory answer the door was opened by one man whilst another stood opposite it ready to shoot me if an enemy. On entering the dining room I found the windows which were on the ground floor barricaded with thick sheets of iron. It appears that the tithes were collected with great severity, and things tithed which was not customary in other parishes; the consequence was that the people endeavoured to shoot the clergyman, firing into his windows and lying in wait for him as he went out, which he never did without an armed man on each side of the road and himself armed with several braces of pistols. He had several narrow escapes and was once desperately wounded.

I had another station in the same county—Mount Shannon. It was a Protestant colony—they were palatines, and I often got myself ferried across to Cameron Fort, another of my out-stations, on the Tipperary side. On one occasion during political excitement, I left Mount Shannon on foot, for the ferry, and had to pass through a number of potato diggers to the river, they allowed me to go halfway before, they began the most hideous shouting and yelling I ever heard before or after. I was alone, but armed with a brace of pistols, it at once struck me that if I proceeded to the river the boatmen might not be willing to put me across, however, my anxiety to get home turned the balance and I proceeded without taking any notice of their noise, and the ferrymen making no difficulty, I passed the river in safety.

On another occasion when crossing from Youghal, on the Nenagh side, to Tomgrany, in Galway, with my ferryman Shawn Baun, and his sister, who pulled one of the oars, the boat a very old one sprung a leak when half way across—the passage was about five miles—his sister a very pretty girl, and when boating bare legged, with the most perfect unconcern thrust her toe into the hole, which, with my assistance baling got us across in safety.

The murders and attempts at murder were of constant occurrence. On one of my visits to my station at Cameron Fort, I found a Mr. Minchin had been murdered the night before; he was thrown into the river, and the time of his murder discovered by the stoppage of his watch. It was said that it was by persons whom he had detected robbing him. If this was the case it was singular that the watch was not taken.

Another murder was perpetrated on the high road, close to Toomavara, another of my out-stations, on the Dublin road. It was at noon day, in sight of the chapel, with the congregation just coming out, who were witnesses of the deed, but made no effort to arrest the perpetrator. It was under suspicion that he had given information of some political affair.

Various attempts were made to shoot my friend Capt. Garvey. He was agent to Lord Bloomfield and Lord Norbury, and was constantly receiving threatening letters, and on several occasions fired at; on one, Mrs. Garvey was sitting beside him in his gig, close at their own gate, when he was fired at from behind a hedge at the side of the road, the ball passed him and struck Mrs. Garvey's bonnet, hurting her with a piece of the wire.

I received some threats myself, but they were never put into execution, which was rather singular, as one of the Roman Catholic clergy called Therry used to make very free with my name, he was considered a great orator, and used to commit his sermons to memory, in so doing he used to walk up and down the garden of a gentleman who lived some doors above my house in Barrack-street, where he supposed himself unseen, and was able to practice his action as well as his speech, the latter was generally violent, but when he wished to turn any one into ridicule, he selected such titles as the following:—He called me the "Carrickfergus ruffian," Miss Cambridge, "the petticoat angel," Mrs. Falkner, the Protestant curate's wife, who wore glasses, "the four-eyed hypocrite," &c,

While living in the street I was near committing a murder myself. One evening while Mrs. Dobbs and myself were sitting at the fire, we heard a rap at the door, then a scream from our housemaid, and a rush of persons into the hall, I snatched up the poker and rushed out, when I saw the maid lying on the stairs, and an immense tall figure just before me, with a crowd of persons behind it, on which I made a blow at its head, which knocked it to pieces and caused a general retreat, it was a person dressed up to represent St. Bridget, and I only struck a broom elevated on a pole.

As I am about it, I may as well give a ghost story of the same locality. The house I lived in was a large one, and for some time various were the reports brought me by the servants and others, that every night the step of a person ascending and descending the stairs was heard, I could not make out what it was, till at last, a circumstance occurred which led me to suspect it was a rat, and I accordingly watched, and finding it was so, followed it down to the kitchen and got it behind the door, but it escaped at the opening. It was shortly afterwards killed by a young kitten, and we had no more ghosts. It was a very large rat, and the manner they light on their four legs on steps of stairs is exactly like a footstep.

My family having increased to eleven children, I thought it would be for their interest to have the price of my commission, so I sold out, and invested the money in the Agricultural Bank, the failure of which and my reduced income placed me in difficulties which gave me some trouble to surmount; about this time, 1841, Captain Rowan, Manager of the Waterford District Lunatic Asylum, asked me to exchange with him, which I agreed to do, he managing matters with the Duke and Lord Lieutenant, so that I had no trouble in the matter.

In the year 1848, being the fiftieth year since the Rebellion of 1798, there was an attempt at outbreak in Ireland, in which the R. C. Chaplain of this Asylum was deeply implicated, and having gone to join the insurgents at Ballingarry, in layman's attire, was taken up in mistake for Dillon, one of the rebel leaders. Doctor Wm. Connolly, our visiting physician, having expressed his disapprobation of their proceeding, he was told by the chaplain that he should have the first shot. All the loyal inhabitants of Waterford were sworn in special constables, I amongst the rest, and we were about forming ourselves into a corps for mutual defence when the overthrow at Ballingarry rendered it unnecessary. On the evening of the outbreak there was a report that the troops which had been withdrawn from Waterford with the exception of the pensioners who were left in charge of the barracks, had been defeated, and almost the whole population were gathered on the quay, I amongst the rest waiting for the mail, by which the news was expected. From the way in which I was eyed, I have little doubt there would have been an outbreak that night if the report had proved true. Pikes had been prepared, patterns having been distributed amongst the people, one of which is in my possession.

Having conducted the duties of the asylum with diligence I have the satisfaction to find that it is not inferior to any other Asylum in the United Kingdom, the recoveries being as numerous and the expenditure less than those with which I have had an opportunity of comparing it.

And now I leave it in 1863 on the most friendly terms with the officers of the institution, who, with the attendants of all classes, have evidenced unfeigned regret at my retirement. I have also to acknowledge the kindness of the Board of Governors and the Members of the County and City Grand Jury, with whom I have been brought into contact from time to time.

Having been in the public service 57 years, I am now desirous of freedom from the cares of official life.

My recollections of the two great men, Nelson and Wellington, who have passed away during the period referred to in this book are fully described in Jeffry's song of Wellington.

Having now glanced over the past sixty years, I look forward with confidence to the future. My hopes are founded on the gracious Revelation of the Almighty. To his servants Daniel and Isaiah, the former giving an outline of the history from his own time to the end of the world, the greater part fulfilled and the latter in his 2nd chapter, 2 to 4 verses describing the thousand years which are to proceed the General Judgement (see *Revelation*, chapter 20;) which may be summed up, as regards war, in the two first verses of Russell's popular song: *There's a Good Time Coming.*

There's a good time coming, boys,
A good time coming;
We may not live to see the day,
But earth shall glisten in the ray,
Of the good time coming
Cannon balls may aid the truth,
But thought's a weapon stronger,
We'll win our battle by its aid—
Wait a little longer.

There's a good time coming, boys,
A good time coming,
War in all men's eyes shall be
A monster of iniquity
In the good time coming;
Nations shall not quarrel then,
To prove which is the stronger,
Nor slaughter men for glory's sake—
Wait a little longer.

An Officer of Fusiliers

Robert Knowles

edited by
Sir Lees Knowles

Contents

Preface	109
Introduction	111
1809	115
1811	119
1812	143
1813	167

Preface

The following lines are from a letter, dated June 28th, 1913, written by Professor C. W. C. Oman, M.A., of All Souls College, Professor of Modern History (Chichele) in Oxford University:

I rejoice to see that there is to be a second edition of these interesting letters, which contain not only a record of the daily life of the 4th Division, with all the details of its toils and marches, but several pieces of narrative of real historical value, especially with regard to the fights at Albuera, Aldea da Ponte, and Salamanca. The writer was a keen and intelligent young soldier, and his letters have not only a special interest for those who are connected with the old 7th, the Royal Fusiliers, but also much that all who care to know about the British army in the Peninsula will be glad to read.

Introduction

These letters were written a hundred years ago by my great-great-uncle, Lieutenant Robert Knowles, and I believe that they, and the notes of Sergeant John Spencer Cooper,[1] are the only contemporary regimental record of the 7th, or Royal, Fusiliers. They came into the possession of his niece, Margaret Mary Knowles, a daughter of James Knowles, who was town clerk of Bolton. They were lent years ago to my father, and he made a copy of them. In 1890, I compared the copy with the originals, which were in a fragile state—moreover, some of them were missing—and this reproduction is from a copy which I made at the time of the comparison. Some of the original letters are again before me. The handwriting shows considerable care, and it is very different from what one would expect in letters written during a campaign. The letters are printed here in their entirety, and the original spelling has been retained. Each letter is folded twice, in long strips, the creases being at right angles to the writing, and the ends of the strips folded together, and sealed in the middle as a rule with red sealing-wax, in several instances bearing, from the impress of a military button, a rose with the legend round it, *Honi soit qui mal y pense.* The address is lengthwise on the back of the sheet. On the letter of July 7th, 1811, is printed in red, square, straight letters, *Maidstone.* On the letter of Au-

1. Published under the title *Fusilier Cooper* by Leonaur.

gust 29th, 1811, is the circular postmark, Portsmouth, *1 Oc. 1. 1811. 73.*; on the letter of Nov. 5th, 1811, is the postmark, *Lisbon, De. 13. 1811. F.*; on the letter of Dec. 31st, 1811, is the postmark, *Lisbon, Ja. 22. 1812*; on the letter of Jan. 20th, 1812, is the postmark, *Lisbon, Feb. 18. 1812*; and, on the letter of Sept. 23rd, 1812, is the postmark, *Lisbon, Se. 23. 1812*. On several letters, printed in black, is the expression *Packet Letter*, with a town after it, such as *Plymouth*, and several of them have *2/5* written upon the face of them. The letter of the Duke of Wellington bears the old blue twopenny stamp, and it is sealed with his crest surrounded by the garter and surmounted by a coronet.

The first of the six volumes of the *History of the War in the Peninsula and in the South of France*, from the year 1807 to the year 1814, by Major-General Sir William Napier, K.C.B., Colonel 27th Regiment, contains the story of the first portion of the war ending in May, 1809, just two months earlier than the first of the letters hereafter printed. That history, full of glowing language and brilliant description, and the admirable, carefully-balanced, and probably more accurate history of the war by Professor Oman, contain all that is essential in connection with this glorious epoch of British military history.

The treaty of Tilsit had given Napoleon a commanding position in Europe, and had brought him directly into conflict with England. France and England were both strong, but the battle of Trafalgar had prevented the invasion of England, and Napoleon therefore proposed to weaken her naval and commercial strength by barring the Continent against English manufactures. It was necessary to do this by French troops. Portugal was virtually an unguarded province of England, whence, and from Gibraltar, English goods passed into Spain. To check this traffic by force was not easy. Spain was to France nearly what Portugal was to England, and the French cause was therefore popular in Spain, and the weak Court of Spain was subservient. Napoleon, accordingly, proposed to place his brother, Joseph Bonaparte, then King of Naples, upon the Spanish Throne, and eventually on July 24th, 1808, he was proclaimed King of Spain and the Indies, becoming, however, the object of a nation's hatred. The volume deals with the principal operations in the eastern and central provinces, and, having shown that the Spaniards, however restless, were unable to throw off the yoke, the writer turns to Portugal, where the invasion was first stayed, and finally forced back by greater strength.

L. K.

July 25th, 1913.

Chapter 1

1809

Old letters, more than old books bring us into direct contact with men of a past age. As we read their exact words and see their hand-writing we seem to know them, and they become real living beings and not figures of imagination, however powerfully portrayed. With soldiers, taking into consideration men of action in every sphere of public life, this is perhaps more true than with any other class, as their work in the world is necessarily more arresting, more striking, more immediately effective.

In these letters, we have an account of stirring events, written within a few days of their occurrence by a young officer who had himself taken part in them. He gives his experiences and impressions modestly, and like most British officers, he is under, rather than over the mark, in stating their value where his own deeds are concerned. When he tells his father that his wounds are slight, the despatches say *severe*. His description of the sufferings of the sick and wounded after Salamanca is not as painful reading as those of the historians who have examined every particle of evidence. The statements made in these letters bear the test of comparison with the official reports, contemporary letters and narratives. As we read, we feel that we are in touch with a man of knowledge and a soldier, whose patriotism took him into the battlefield. He had not the inducement of monetary reward;

for, after the manner of his kind, he had to pay, and pay heavily, to serve his country.

Such an example should not be forgotten, or the memory of heroism and of self-sacrifice be buried in oblivion For a well-informed, patriotic, nation, time brightens rather than dims the lustre of the fame of soldiers who have fallen in battle, and the glories of the War in the Peninsula have been revived by the series of centenaries that have been celebrated since 1908. A nation or country forgetful of its past history is one that is doomed to defeat and decay.

The year 1809 opened badly for England. An illustrious soldier was struck down in the very moment of his victory. Sir John Moore had led the army committed to his care with consummate skill. His retreat on Corunna accomplished its purpose, and justified his foresight The Emperor Napoleon at the head of his hitherto victorious legions was drawn from Madrid, whither fate decreed that he was never to return. The soldiers who fought under Moore returned to England worn out by privation and hardships. Within a few months they were again hastened to South Beveland on what was known as the Walcheren Expedition, and then, without accomplishing any useful purpose, they returned to England decimated by fever, many dying, and a large proportion of the survivors remaining for some years in a state of convalescence. Ireland at that time absorbed an army of no less than 60,000 men. England was garrisoned largely by the constitutional force, the Militia. One regiment, the Royal Lancaster, was embodied and quartered at Bristol, and the writer of these letters joined it there in July, 1809.

Robert Knowles was the fourth son of Robert Knowles, of Quarlton and Eagley Bank, Little Bolton, in the County of Lancaster. He was born on April 4th, 1790, and in 1809 he was gazetted as lieutenant in the Royal Lancaster Regiment.

The first letter to his father gives a glimpse of the old coaching-days, a journey of thirteen hours from Manchester to Birmingham, a crowded mail-coach necessitating the delay of one night, and then an all-day journey to Bristol. The letter is dated Bristol, July 25th, 1809, and the reader will notice the coincidence that the day was a fatal one for the writer.

To his father Robert Knowles

Bristol, July 25th, 1809—I now sit down to inform you of my safe arrival at Bristol. I left Manchester at half-past one o'clock on Saturday morning, accompanied by Lieutenant Bottomley, and we arrived at Birmingham at half-past two o'clock Saturday evening, from which town the mail was filled, so that we were obliged to stop one night at Birmingham. We immediately took seats in the stagecoach, which sets off early on Sunday morning, and arrived at this place at nine o'clock on Sunday evening. We had a very pleasant and agreeable journey.

On Monday morning we waited upon the Colonel, and I delivered Captain Mason's letter to his friend, Lieutenant Bythesea, by whom I have been very handsomely received. He introduced me to the officers of the regiment, who appear to be very agreeable gentlemen. Lieutenant Bythesea's best respects to Captain Mason, and please to inform him that he has a little boy. Please to return Captain Mason my sincere thanks for the kindness shown unto me. Mr. Bottomley and myself have taken lodgings in College Place, which consists of two bedrooms and one parlour, for which we are to pay 21s. per week.

Bristol is a very large and pleasant city, and the docks are full of shipping in consequence of the embargo. We have very bad news from abroad, but hope it will be better than what is represented. On Monday night there was a fatal duel in the French prison near this place between two of the prisoners. The weapons they fought with were two pieces of broken files, about six inches long, sharpened and tied at the end of sticks. They fought a considerable time, when one of them was stuck to the heart. If you do see Mr. Orrell desire him to join as soon as possible, as I think it would be much better for him, as he will have more to learn than he is aware of.

I will write again in the course of a week. I am very anxious to hear how my grandfather is, and I do hope this will find you and all the family in good health. Please to remember me to all enquiring friends.

P.S.—I hope you will not delay writing to me. Please to address—Lieutenant Knowles, 1st R.L. Militia, Bristol. In haste and a bad pen.

There is here a long break of two years in the letters which have been preserved. The next is a short note from Hull, written on May 25th, 1811, when the writer was in daily expectation of receiving a commission in the regular army.

CHAPTER 2

1811

To his father Robert Knowles

Hull, 25th May, 1811—As I gave you reason to expect me
at home about this time, I think it my duty to inform you
that I cannot leave the regiment until my name appears in the
Gazette, which I hope will be in a few days, after which I will
lose no time in repairing home. We have no news here worth
committing to paper, particularly as I am very soon expecting
to see you.

The 7th Royal Fusiliers

On May 7th, 1811, Robert Knowles was appointed lieutenant in the 7th Royal Fusiliers, then, as now, one of the
most distinguished regiments in the army; and, within a
month, he was at Maidstone where he had joined the depot of his regiment.
This letter tells the home-circle of his arrival, and gives
some information about the uniform and expenses of
those days. Six guineas for the stamp on a first commission was a heavy tax for a young officer. As is not
even now-a-days unusual, the tailor came in for the chief
share of the spoil, with a bill of £20 for a regimental coat
and wings.

Maidstone, 23rd June, 1811—I arrived at London about ten o'clock on the evening of the 19th, and at Maidstone on the evening of the 21st, where I was well received by the commanding officer and officers of the regiment at present with the depot. There is a draft of four hundred men and nine officers (including myself) ordered to be in readiness to proceed to Portsmouth to embark for Portugal on the 25th inst., but we have not yet received our route, and I think it probable it will be put off a few days longer.

I wish you to send me by the Defiance coach from the Bridgewater Arms, Manchester, which leaves at four o clock in the evening, my large box (if it is yet arrived from Hull), with my two old regimental coats, white pantaloons, two pair blue pantaloons, the best I have got, two sashes, sword knot, cocked hat, shoes, pair of boots, linen, bed-linen, two black silk handkerchiefs, paper-case, and any other things that I have got which you think will be of use to me. I am very sorry I did not see my brother Chadwick at Manchester, and it hurt me much to leave my sister alone, but I hope she very soon found him.

When we receive our route I will write you by that day's post. We are seven days' march from Portsmouth. I am going to London tomorrow to stop a few days, where I intend providing myself with everything that is necessary. I am under the necessity of requesting you will send me £30 by return of post (underneath you have an estimate of my expenses), which I hope will be the last sum I shall trouble you for until my return from abroad.

Estimate of my Expense	£	s	d
Regimental Coat and Wings	20	0	0
Sabre	4	4	0
Cap	6	6	0
Large Blue Pantaloons and Chain	2	5	0

Three Pair Shoes and Gaiters	2	14	0
Belt and Breast Plate	2	0	0
Commission	6	6	0
Plate			
Sundries			
Total	£43	15	0

The above is the lowest estimate, and I am having my old coat cut down for a service jacket, which will be an expense of three or four pounds in gold lace, &c.

My address in London, where I shall remain until Saturday next: Lieutenant Knowles, 7th Royal Fusiliers, No. 28, Suffolk Street, Charing Cross, London.

Directions for my large box: Lieutenant Knowles, 7th Royal Fusiliers, Maidstone, to be forwarded by the coach from the Golden Cross, Charing Cross, London.

P.S.—If you can send my box by the Defiance coach on Thursday I shall receive it at London. In that case, direct it to be left at the coach office till called for. Please mention the direction in your letter, which I hope you will not fail to send by return of post.

I intended writing yesterday, but there was no post from this town with speed.

I have this moment received a parcel from home, also a letter from my brother. Therefore, it will be unnecessary sending me bed linen or anything else, unless I find it necessary to write for them when I get to Portsmouth, but I hope you will not fail sending me the sum I have wrote for by return of post, after seeing Captain Robinson's letter.

Lieutenant Knowles was in London on June 29th, 1811, and the victory to which he refers in his letter of that date must have been the Battle of Albuera, fought on May 16th. Marshal Beresford, and not Wellington, commanded the Allies.

Rumour and false intelligence were very prevalent in

those days. The distance, the difficulties of communication, the uncertainty of sailing-ships, the stories circulated by interested parties, both friends and foes, all tended to create fiction, sometimes alarming, and often harassing.

TO HIS BROTHER CHADWICK KNOWLES

London, June 29th, 1811—I have just received yours of the 27th instant, enclosing a £30 draft and one pound note, for which I return my father my sincere thanks.

You have given me Mr. John Woods' address, but it was unnecessary, having called upon him twice, but have nothing to thank him for but mere civility. We have no further information respecting our march, but expect it daily. You mention my sister's letter that she wrote me. I shall take an opportunity of answering it in a few days. I intend returning to Maidstone on Monday next. I should have deferred writing until tomorrow, having received your letter so late in the evening, but for a report there is in Town that there has been a very severe action in Spain, in which our army was crowned with victory, but with very severe loss. Report says that Lord Wellington has lost a leg, and that Marshall Beresford is killed, but the French army is entirely dispersed. It is believed by many people in the Town, but I am very doubtful, as it is a French account, and it is unusual for them to spread reports to their disadvantage. I have not time to write anything more unless I lose the advantage of to-night's post.

> To his sister are given particulars of the final marching orders, and the keen spirit of the soldier is shown in his desire to take his place in the field against the enemies of his country.

TO HIS SISTER MISS KNOWLES

Maidstone, July 7th, 1811—I received yours of the 20th ult. in due time, and am glad to see you give yourself credit for not opening my letters, but I still think that a female's curiosity will not be satisfied until she knows the contents. You say that you have heard a report that the officers of our regiment are returning from Spain, but I am happy to inform you that there is not the least foundation for the report. So far from it that we nine officers and 400 men have received our route to march for Portsmouth on Wednesday and Thursday next, there to embark to join our gallant comrades in Spain. I am ordered to march with the 2nd Division on Thursday, and shall arrive at Portsmouth on Wednesday, the 17th instant, where I expect to hear from home on my arrival with a parcel containing the remainder of my shirts, nightshirts, stockings, bed-linen, military books, French books, brace of small pistols with the moulds, and portmanteaus. I am induced to write for those things, our regiment having a store at Lisbon, where I intend leaving most of my baggage, as I can at any time send for everything that is necessary to that place. I spent my time very pleasantly in London, where I remained about eight days. I was in a private lodging-house along with an officer of our regiment, who knows a great deal of the town, and he was so obliging as to go with me wherever I pleased. I wish you to forward the parcel by the coach on the 12th or 13th, with directions to be left till called for. Before I take leave of Old England I will write to my father, and every future opportunity that occurs I shall take great pleasure in writing to my friends in Lancashire. I shall endeavour to see Lieutenant Woods in Spain; if his friends have anything to send to him I should be happy to take charge of it.

P.S.—It is dinner-hour, therefore must conclude.

A march of seven days brought Lieutenant Knowles and the detachment of the 7th Royal Fusiliers from Maidstone to Hilsea Barracks, Portsmouth, on July 17th, 1811. The embarkation took place on the following day. Adverse winds detained the fleet of transports for a week at Spithead, where the following letter was written on July 24th, 1811.

Spithead, July 24th, 1811—I take the latest opportunity of addressing you on leaving for a short time my much beloved country. I must commence with our march from Maidstone to Portsmouth, which was a very pleasant one. We passed through Tunbridge, Tunbridge Wells, East Grinstead, Horsham, Petworth, Chichester to Hilsea Barracks, near Portsmouth, where we arrived on the 17th, and embarked early on the morning of the 18th, in the *Matilda* Transport No. 68. We immediately dropped down to Spithead, where we have since remained, weather bound, but there is now a fair wind, and we expect to sail in the course of the day. I have received a trunk from home. Enclosed I found a kind letter from you. My brother's letter is also come to hand, in which he informs me that I might expect to see Mr. Orrel in Portsmouth. He is arrived and on board the *Arethusa* transport, but I have not yet seen him. I went on board that vessel yesterday, but he was on shore. If possible I will see him in the course of the day, as my brother informs me he has a portmanteau in charge for me. There is a large fleet of transports going to Portugal from this place, with about three thousand troops on board. If we have a quick passage we shall be a very seasonable supply for Lord Wellington. Our detachment is about 370 strong, in high spirits, and anxious to join their brave comrades in Spain.

27th—The wind is now fair, and the fleet is now getting under weigh. We have no news, therefore must conclude. Trusting I shall have the pleasure of seeing my dear father, brothers, and sisters all in good health on my return,

P.S.—I have seen Mr. Orrel; he is in good health. I forgot to say that the wind changed on the 24th, therefore delayed finishing my letter for a few days. You shall hear from me on my arrival at Lisbon.

The Fleet was compelled to put into Falmouth, and the last letter he was fated to write within sight of his native land was written from the Cornish port. It is easy to imagine the impatience of 10 officers and 370 men, "cabined, cribbed, confined," for sixteen days in a sailing transport, between Spithead and Falmouth, with little comfort and indifferent food. Biscuit and salt beef was then the staple ration of our soldiers, and even that was not always in a sound and wholesome condition. In those days such meat, supplied for long voyages, was called *junk*, because it resembled old rope-ends in hardness and toughness. But, there was in some measure compensation in a quick trip to Lisbon, as twelve days was good sailing in the early years of the nineteenth century.

To his father Robert Knowles

Falmouth Harbour, Aug. 9th, 1811, on board Matilda Transport—You will see in the public prints an account of our arrival at this place. We were obliged to put in by contrary winds on the morning of the 2nd inst. I have delayed writing, expecting hourly to set sail, when I hope we shall be more fortunate. The fleet for Lisbon consists of about seventy sail. We are on board the fastest sailer and the finest transport in the fleet. Contrary to my expectation I have not experienced the least sea-sickness, and I am happy to say our men continue in the best state of health. You will see in this month's army list how fortunate I am in my appointment, as there are now eight lieutenants junior to me. I saw Mr. Orrel in Falmouth on Wednesday last. He told me that he had wrote home and mentioned that he had seen me. The last accounts from our regiment, the 2nd Battalion were under orders for England, but I hope the orders will be countermanded. On my arrival in Portugal, I hope I shall have the pleasure of receiving a letter from you.

P.S.—We are now under sail. *Adieu!* Please to direct: Lieutenant Knowles, 7th Royal Fusiliers, with the army in Portugal.

Two letters from Portugal describe the impression which Lisbon, the capital, made on the soldiers, upon their arrival there.

To his father Robert Knowles

To HIS FATHER ROBERT KNOWLES

Lisbon, August 24th, 1811—I am happy to inform you of my arrival at this place on the 21st inst. We had a very good passage from Falmouth, and landed at Lisbon on the 22nd inst. Our men are quartered in the convent of Carmo, but we expect daily to march to the army. Our detachment was very fortunate in leaving England before the arrival of our 2nd Battalion, which has left Lisbon about three weeks. I was very sorry to see so many of our brave fellows sick and wounded in the hospitals at Lisbon and Belem. A great many of our officers are at Lisbon sick and wounded, many of them without hopes of recovery. A Lieutenant Jones, of our regiment, died yesterday. The last accounts from our army they were blockading Ciudad Rodrigo—our regiment is attached to the Light Division. To give you a description of Lisbon—the town is well built, and stands on the rise of a hill, but the streets smell abominably. The filthy inhabitants throw their dirt into the streets as soon as it is dark, and they pay little attention to clearing it away in the morning. I will return the letters for Lieutenant Woods and Richard Booth, of the 48th Regiment, the first opportunity, understanding they have left this country for England. I will write to you as soon as we join the regiment. I am informed that we are to march through the most barren country, laid waste by the army. We have no news here, and have not heard from England since our arrival. Be so good as to remember me to all enquiring friends, particularly to my dear sisters and brothers, and believe me,

P.S.—I am sorry I have delayed writing until half an hour before the sailing of the packet, but lost no time in writing after receiving the information, therefore you must excuse all mistakes and the shortness of the letter. We are about 250 miles from the army.

To his father Robert Knowles

Lisbon, 29th August, 1811—I avail myself of this opportunity of forwarding the enclosed letters to Mr. Wood, understanding that both his son and Richard Booth are returned to England with the 2nd Battalion of the 48th. We embark to-morrow morning to sail up the Mondego as far as Coimbra, so that we shall be a few days at sea. I mentioned to you in my last letter that Lisbon is a dirty town; it is also infested with a multitude of dogs, which no person owns. On account of their infernal howling (all the night) I could not sleep for several nights after my arrival. I wrote in my last that our men were quartered in the convent of Carmo. The officers are all billeted in private houses. We have our regular rations of beef and biscuits, but the meat we have is so poor that it would be burnt if exposed for sale in Bolton market. At present we are in a town where there is plenty of good things. When we leave, John Bull must give up his idea of good living. I have not seen Mr. Orrel since my arrival in Lisbon, but hear that he marches in a few days to join his regiment, which is with General Hill's Division near Badajos. I am apprehensive that the officers of this detachment, after our arrival at the army, will be ordered back to England to join our 2nd Battalion, which is to be quartered in Yorkshire, either at York, Beverley, or Richmond. Yesterday a very fine vessel was burnt in the Tagus. She had been used as a store ship. Our regimental stores were taken out of her a few days ago, but I hear the heavy baggage of three other regiments is entirely destroyed. The last accounts from the army, our Light troops were advancing, and the 3rd Division had invested Ciudad Rodrigo. The weather is very hot, but I hope our marches to join the army will be made in the night as much as possible. I am daily expecting to hear from home, and hope you will often write and give me all the news you can. Give my love to my brothers and sisters, and remember me to all enquiring friends.

I send this per favour of Mr. Pennie, of our regiment, who returns to England in consequence of severe wounds.

After a delay of one week at Lisbon, the detachments started to join the army under Lord Wellington. The party of the 7th Royal Fusiliers, in strength nearly equal to half a battalion, was commanded by Lieutenant Charles Barrington, a young officer of three years' service. This is an illustration of the youth of the soldiers who were sent to fill the depleted ranks of Wellington's army. Another officer, Lieutenant Cameron, who was serving with this draft, records in his Journal that "the men were so young, and were worked so hard, that before the winter was over, 300 had either died or been sent home to England". The following letter gives the line of march, and, considering the times, and that it was written in a cantonment without any facilities for writing, it is a remarkably good letter.

To his father Robert Knowles

Aldea de Bisboa, Oct. 7th, 1811—I have now the satisfaction of addressing you from a Spanish town, after a long and fatiguing march through Portugal. I wrote you last when on the point of sailing for the river Mondego, where we anchored after three days' passage on the 4th Sept., and immediately landed at Figueras. On the 8th, we commenced our march for the army. We passed through Monte Mor and Perona to Coimbra, where we arrived on the 11th. On the 14th we proceeded on our march through Algacia, Moita, Galleces, Meneca, Sampayo, Celonio, Bacasal, Castell Boni, Navo de Vene to Fuentes de Quinaldo (the headquarters of Lord Wellington and also of General Cole, who commands the 4th Division of the army), where we arrived on the morning of the 25th. At the time our advanced brigade was engaged with the enemy. The Fusilier Brigade had marched about half an hour when we arrived to cover the retreat of the advance, the particulars of which you will see in the Gazette. Our regiment advanced in line with the 23rd and 48th in close column on each flank, when, having accomplished their object, they gradually returned to their position, where we had the pleasure of joining them.

Robert Knowles reached Fuente Guinaldo on September 25th, 1811, and it may perhaps be of assistance to the reader if an outline be given of the position of the army in Portugal, and of the 7th Royal Fusiliers at this time.

On May 16th, 1811, the battle of Albuera was won by the British soldier, and not by the general-ship of the commanders of the allied troops engaged. The hill of Albuera is celebrated in military histories. Imagine six thousand British soldiers fighting for four hours against heavy odds to gain its crest, a heavy rain falling and sometimes obscuring the enemy from their view, and the water-courses of the hill-side coloured with blood! Of the six thousand, only fifteen hundred reached the crest of the hill unwounded. A memorable example of British endurance and pluck.

The 7th Royal Fusiliers and the 23rd Fusiliers formed the Fusilier Brigade of the 4th Division, and in a crisis of the battle these soldiers, under the leadership of Lieutenant-Colonel Sir William Myers of the 7th, forced their way up the hill, struck and shattered a division of the French in flank, and recaptured six guns. Of those who fought at Albuera it would be invidious to select any regiment, or section; but, the two Fusilier Regiments were conspicuous. Of the 7th Royal Fusiliers, with the laurels of Albuera fresh upon them, Robert Knowles had now become a member, joining it when it was actually in action, under the immediate direction of the greatest commander of the day. Lord Wellington was then blockading Ciudad Rodrigo, and his headquarters were at Fuente Guinaldo. For six weeks, he had blockaded the fortress, and, the garrison being in straits for food, Marshal Marmont resolved to pass in a convoy. With an army of sixty thousand men, this was not a difficult operation, his adversary not being in a position to fight a general action. Wellington, however, drew in his forces which were scattered in and about El Bodon and Fuente Guinaldo. By so doing, he compelled Marmont to bring up his full strength before the revictualling of the beleaguered fortress, which was accomplished on September 24th. On the following day, General Montbrun with fourteen battalions of infantry and a strong force of cavalry advanced on Fuente Guinaldo, and thus began at El Bodon, six miles away, the action which was at its height when Lieutenant Knowles and his detachment arrived at Fuente Guinaldo.

The 3rd Division held the centre of the allied position at El Bodon and Pastores, which were within three miles of Ciudad Rodrigo. The Light Division was on the right at Martiago on the Vadillo river, the 6th Division and a brigade of cavalry held the left. The pivot on which they all turned was Fuente Guinaldo, and at that spot was posted the 4th Division with which the 7th Royal Fusiliers were serving.

At daybreak on September 25th, General Montbrun, with fourteen battalions of infantry and three brigades of cavalry, crossed the Águeda river, and attacked at once our line of cavalry picquets on the plain in the vicinity of El Bodon. The Frenchmen were met by the "fighting 3rd" division under General Sir Thomas Picton. Taken in an exposed and isolated position and with his flank turned, Sir Thomas Picton retired from El Bodon and its vineyards, moving his column slowly across the plain, and, although repeatedly charged by the enemy's cavalry, and fired at by six guns on his flank and rear, coolly and skilfully withdrew his division. This retreat for six miles was a fine exhibition of nerve and calm self-possession on the part of the Commander, and of steadiness under fire on the part of his officers and men.

When Wellington discovered the object of the French Commander, he sent the 5th Fusiliers, the 77th British, and the 21st Portuguese Regiments, and some artillery, to occupy the hill over which ran the road to Fuente Guinaldo. The French cavalry attacked the hill with great vigour; but, they were again and again driven down the upper slopes. Montbrun brought up his artillery and soon made an impression, his cavalry capturing some of our guns. Meanwhile, our cavalry, by charging too far, became entangled in the vineyards. In this crisis, the 5th Fusiliers performed one of those extraordinary feats of valour which were not infrequent in the campaigns under Wellington. Led by Major Ridge, the 5th Fusiliers dashed at the French cavalry, and, sending them flying, recaptured the guns. It recalls the rout of the cavalry at Minden by six British regiments of infantry.

Lord Wellington ordered a general retirement to the plain below, where the 5th and 77th formed one square, and repulsed time after time the cavalry that charged them. All the forces, being re-united, now retired across the plain to the position at Fuente Guinaldo, which Wellington had defended by entrenchments and three redoubts. It was during this retirement that the Fusilier Brigade— the 7th and 23rd Fusiliers and the 48th Regiment—of the 4th Division came up and covered the withdrawal referred to by Lieutenant Knowles in his letter of October 7th, where he says—

When we arrived the Fusilier Brigade had marched about half an hour to cover the retreat of the advance .... Our regiment advanced in line with the 23rd and 48th in close column on each flank, when, having accomplished their object, they gradually returned to their position, where we had the pleasure of joining them.

There is one incident in the combat at El Bodon, mentioned by Sir William Napier, which is particularly worthy of note:

> It was in one of the cavalry encounters that a French officer, in the act of striking at the gallant Felton Harvey of the 14th Dragoons, perceived that he had only one arm, and with a rapid movement brought down his sword into a salute, and passed on.

Such were the courtesies between gallant men of both nations in this war.

Wellington in remaining at Fuente Guinaldo accepted a great risk which Napier describes as "above the rules of war." With a disposable force of 14,000 men and in a moderate position, he confronted 60,000 men, remaining on the spot for thirty-six hours rather than abandon the famous Light Division. That risk was brought about by the deliberate failure of General Robert Craufurd to obey a written order to fall back upon Fuente Guinaldo. General Robert Craufurd, the ablest Lieutenant who ever served under Wellington, was the Commander of the Light Division, which was probably the most perfect fighting unit of Wellington's armies. Receiving the order before 3 p.m. he marched only four miles, thus jeopardizing the safety of the whole force. Two regiments of Picton's Division that were at Pastores, cut off by Montbrun's turning movement, made a march of fifteen hours and reached Fuente Guinaldo at night. Craufurd, without danger, could have done likewise. Wellington took the risk. Craufurd, however, was blind to the offence of disregarding rders from his chief: for, he gave him the simple assurance that he was in no danger. "But it was, through your conduct that there was danger," was the calm and stern reply.

Still oblivious to his fault, Craufurd said to his Staff, referring to his chief, "he is d——d crusty to-day."

The letter of Oct. 7th, continues, and describes the position at this moment:

We remained under arms during the night. The Fusiliers formed the left of the line, where it was supposed the enemy would make their principal attack, which was fully expected early in the morning. Lord Wellington remained with us all the night and following day, while the enemy were amusing us by manoeuvring in our front and bringing up their numerous reinforcements. About sunset Lord Wellington left us, and immediately the army was on the move. Our regiment brought up the rear of the division, and marched about eleven o'clock, and did not halt until eleven o'clock the following morning at Aldea de Ponte.

At midnight on the 26th, the army was in retreat, and by a skilful movement, Wellington united the whole twelve miles distant from Fuente Guinaldo, and behind the Villar Mayor.

As the next combat is the first in which Lieutenant Knowles received his baptism of fire, it may be of interest to give the disposition of the various divisions. The right was held by the 5th Division at Aldea Velha, the 4th and Light Divisions and a cavalry brigade were in the centre in front of the village at Alfayates, and behind these, as a reserve, were the 3rd and 7th Divisions. On the left of the latter division was a convent, whence the line was prolonged by two Portuguese brigades, the 6th Division and cavalry brigade bringing the line to an end at Bismula.

In the front of the village of Aldea da Ponte, but leaning towards Furcalhous on the right of the position, was a line of our cavalry picquets. Following in close pursuit, the French came up in force on the morning of the 27th, drove in the cavalry picquets, and by ten o'clock were in possession of Aldea da Ponte.

At noon they attacked General Pakenham's brigade of the Fourth Division, composed of the Fusilier Brigade of the 7th Royal Fusiliers, and the 23rd Fusiliers, and the 48th Regiment, which was posted on a range of heights. Wellington rode up at the critical moment, as he so frequently did, and directed the 7th to charge in line, supporting them on each flank with a Portuguese regiment in column. Down they went, sending helter-skelter before them, the French, who then, entering a wood, tried to turn the position; but, they were thwarted by our artillery. Wellington, thereupon, acted on the offensive, and sent the 23rd and a Portuguese regiment against the left of the French. They were successful, and the village was once more in the possession of the allies. A second party of the enemy coming up joined those who had attacked the village, making a fresh combined attack at five o'clock, and Aldea da Ponte was theirs for the second time. General Pakenham at the head of the two Fusilier Regiments drove them out again; but, as the enemy were in considerable force, and the light failing, and, as he knew that Wellington had fixed upon other ground for fighting a battle, he left Aldea da Ponte and re-occupied his position of the morning.

A description of the fight appears in the letter of October 7th, 1811. It is the account of a young enthusiastic officer, fighting with his regiment, thrilled with all the excitement and glow of a first battle. The letter of Oct. 7th continues:

About one o'clock the enemy made their appearance. It was a beautiful sight to see our cavalry skirmishing with them, but before their superior numbers they gradually retired upon us. Our Light Company, with the Light Companies of the 23rd, 48th, and a company of Germans, acted in our front. Our regiment was formed in square to receive their numerous cavalry, which were rapidly advancing. The 23rd and 48th were also formed in square, a short distance upon our right, and about three thousand Portuguese were formed in line on some rising ground in our rear. Our cavalry, about 2,000, formed on our left. This was the whole of the force we had to oppose to them on that day. Our light infantry gave a good account of the enemy's cavalry, which retired in confusion. Several columns of infantry continued to advance rapidly when we were suddenly ordered to form line. The fatigues of the night were forgot when Lord Wellington ordered the Fusiliers to charge the enemy. We advanced steadily against a heavy column of Imperial Guards, but they, perceiving our intention, retired in double quick time. Our light infantry poured in a dreadful fire amongst them, and numbers of them lay dead and dying on the field. They attempted to form on a rising ground opposite, where our artillery did great execution. Our cavalry and light infantry pursued them several miles, and were supported by a regiment of Portuguese Cacadores. We naturally concluded that we should see no more of them that day, but the rascals had formed a plan to surprise our light infantry. About six o'clock we heard our light infantry very warmly engaged with them. General Packenham ordered the Fusiliers to fall in, and immediately marched us in the direction ot the fire. My captain was just gone on picket, so that I had the honour of commanding a company in action. We advanced in double quick time, and arrived when they had nearly surrounded the light infantry. Our right wing was ordered to charge, and to describe the eagerness of the men to close with them is impossible. General Packenham led us on (he is our lieutenant-colonel—under such a man cowards would fight). Balls were flying about our ears like a hail-storm. He took off his hat, waved it in the air, and cried out "Lads! Remember the Fusiliers!"

The huzza that followed intimidated the French, and they ran too fast for our bayonets, but our fire mowed them down by dozens. We pursued them to the skirts of a wood, when we were ordered to retire. Our retiring encouraged the enemy, and the wood appeared like a flame with the fire they opened upon us. We retired in good order, the enemy not knowing the small number of men we had in the field, or they must inevitably have cut us to pieces, as we were afterwards informed by prisoners and deserters that they had eight thousand men in the wood, and the whole of the force we opposed to them did not exceed 500 men. The four companies we charged them with did not exceed 200 men. We had now time to look after our friends. We had four officers wounded, but none of them seriously. Many poor fellows fell on my right and left. One ball grazed my cap, another cut my canteen-strap in two, but I am happy to say there was not one billeted upon my body.

During the night, Wellington withdrew his army to a strong position on the Coa, which offered a very narrow frontage for attack. Marmont did not venture to test the strength of his opponent, but contented himself by placing a fresh Garrison in Ciudad Rodrigo. Wellington cantoned his army along both banks of the Coa, giving them a much-needed rest, at the same time sending the Light Division and a cavalry brigade to watch Ciudad Rodrigo. The letter of Oct. 7th ends, and gives the precise details of the movement of the writer's regiment:

On the morning of the 28th the greatest part of our army was concentrated, but the enemy had received too good a lesson from our division to follow the whole army. We remained two nights in a large chestnut grove. We marched on the 1st, 2nd, and arrived at Alameda on the 3rd instant. On the 5th we marched to this place, Aldea de Bisboa. The whole army, it is supposed, is in winter quarters, as rest is now absolutely necessary to recruit the army. In the sick returns of last month there was upwards of 22,000 British, and about one-half of the Portuguese army.

The following letter, which is chiefly of a personal and domestic nature, gives the writer's estimation of the Spaniards and the Portuguese:

To his father Robert Knowles

Aldea de Bisboa, Oct. 8th, 1811—I write to you the first opportunity after the marches, counter-marches, and hard fighting we have had. I intended writing immediately after my arrival at the army, but found it impossible to procure paper. They were all in such a state of confusion, and all our baggage was sent into the rear. I received mine on the 30th in the Chestnut Grove, and to-morrow the first mail for England leaves the army. I was very unfortunate in my baggage being left behind. All the officers of the detachment were in the same situation; when we received it, it had been pillaged. I had 35 dollars taken out of my portmanteau, besides a quantity of linen. The dollars was the balance due to the company I commanded. I am therefore under the necessity of again calling upon your generosity for the sum of ten pounds to be paid into the hands of Messrs. Greenwood & Co., army agents, on account of Lieutenant H. F. Devey, with instructions to them to write to Mr. Devey the day they receive it. He has kindly offered to lend me the sum. Hope you will remit it to Messrs. Greenwood & Co. immediately, and write to me by the same post. I am much disappointed at not hearing from home since I left England, but suppose the reason to be that you are not aware the postage of all letters must be paid in England, which are going abroad. I will now give you a little of the country we passed through. From Figueras to Coimbra is a very fine corn country, and well cultivated. Coimbra is a large town, and has not suffered so much from the French as all the other towns. From Coimbra to Celorico it is a very rocky and mountainous country, but the valleys are full of olive trees, and the mountains covered with vineyards. We marched in the track the French army retreated. They have destroyed all the villages, and there is scarcely a house with a roof on. The country appears quite depopulated. The little I have seen of the Spaniards I like much better than the Portuguese; they are a much finer race of people, and take more pains to keep themselves clean. Their land is much better cultivated, and the French have not destroyed any of their villages. I must conclude, begging that you will write immediately on the receipt of this.

Mr. Devey's address which I wish you to send to—Messrs. Greenwood and Co., Lieutenant H. F. Devey, 7th Fusiliers, British army, Portugal or Spain.

P.S.—I promised to write to my Couzin John Lomax, but have entirely forgot his address. Please to give it me in your next. If anything particularly interesting occurs I will write home. Lieutenant Wray, of our regiment, desires to be remembered to his brother, who is at Dr. Moor's.

A month elapses, when another letter, written to his father, tells of the movements of the army in a comparatively quiet interlude:

To his father Robert Knowles

Villa de Saya, Nov. 5th, 1811—I wrote you last from Aldea de Bisboa on the 8th ult., and on the 12th we were moved to this village, where we remained quiet until Saturday last, when we were suddenly ordered to march in the direction of Quinaldo (you will recollect it is the place I mentioned in my last as having joined our regiment). We were all of us ignorant of the business we were going upon until we arrived at the end of our march, when we were much mortified to hear that John Bull was too late, and we were ordered to march back to our old quarters on the following day. It was intended that our division should intercept a large convoy of stores that was going to the relief of Ciudad Rodrigo, escorted by about five thousand men, but the enemy had accomplished their purpose the day before we marched. There has nothing interesting occurred since my last letter. You will see in the papers an account of the capture by the Spaniards of the Governor of Ciudad Rodrigo. He was marched prisoner through this village. The French lately murdered some Spanish prisoners, and they naturally retaliated by murdering some Frenchmen that fell into their hands a few days ago. They have also detected a French spy, and were so kind as to make us a present of a hind quarter, which is hung up a short distance from my billet. A few days ago I visited Almieda. The town is destroyed, and the fortifications are very much injured, but Lord Wellington is now repairing the works. On Sunday I had a very fine view of Ciudad Rodrigo, as I walked within three miles of the town, but hope to have a nearer inspection the ensuing spring. I am sorry to say I have not received a letter from home since I left England, but am daily expecting that pleasure. We have great news from General Hill's army, but you will see the particulars before we have them, as the only accounts we expect to receive will be through the English papers. On the receipt of the first letter from home I shall again write.

The Governor of Ciudad Rodrigo, to whose capture reference is made, was General Renaud, who had imprudently left a fortress with a weak escort, and he and his whole party, with 200 head of cattle, were captured by the Spanish cavalry under Julian Sanchez. The loss of the cattle was of more serious consequence to the Garrison than the loss of the Governor. The position of the Commander was taken by the next senior officer, but, the loss of the cattle could not be made good.

Then, as now, armies in the field, fighting in an extended area, had less knowledge of what was occurring in other divisions than had people living at a distance.

General Hill was operating at this time in Estremadura, and his swift and brilliant surprise and dispersion of the force under General Gerard in Arroyo dos Molinos, deservedly established his reputation as a Commander; this is the "great news" mentioned in the last paragraph but one of the letter of November 5th. In this affair, out of 3,000, only 600 Frenchmen escaped.

In the letter of December 3rd, 1811, there is no exaggeration of the hardships and privations of the army at that time. Napier says, "the pay of the army was three months in arrears, and the supplies, brought up with difficulty, were very scanty; half and quarter rations were often served, and sometimes the troops were without any bread for three days consecutively." The labour of preparing for a siege was arduous. It was mid-winter and the cantonments were unhealthy from incessant rain. It is not surprising, therefore, that there were 20,000 men in hospital.

To his father Robert Knowles

Barba de Porca, Dec. 3rd, 1811—I am happy to acknowledge the receipt of my brother's letter of the 30th Sept. Since I last wrote you on the 4th ult. we have had some very severe marches. On the 11th, four companies of our regiment marched from Villa de Serva to this village, which is situated upon the Aqueda. Here is the celebrated pass by which the French garrison of Almeida escaped. The river runs rapidly, and the rocks on each side are tremendous. It is really astonishing how they succeeded. On the 23rd, in the morning, we had only ten minutes' notice to march in the direction of Ciudad Rodrigo. We joined our regiment in the evening at Gallegas, after a march of twenty-five miles. Early in the morning we proceeded on our march to camp Ello, a miserable village about six miles on the right of Ciudad Rodrigo. Near this place the enemy must pass if they relieved that fortress. Here we remained until the 29th, when we were ordered to return to our old quarters. The five days we were at camp Ello we only received one pound of biscuit, and fatigue partys were ordered into the woods to gather acorns as a substitute for bread. In this starving state we had only twenty cottages to quarter seven hundred men. You will agree with me when I say very few men in England would envy our situation. On the 1st instant two officers from each regiment were ordered to examine the passes over the Aqueda, so as to enable them to conduct the different Regiments in the most expeditious manner to any point that may be required. The enemy's convoys are now at Salamanca, waiting a favourable opportunity of proceeding to the relief of Ciudad Rodrigo, but I believe they will find it a difficult matter unless they collect their immense army. The deserters from the enemy are very numerous, particularly from Ciudad Rodrigo. The morning we marched to this village we met one officer and twenty-eight men; those from Ciudad Rodrigo say that the garrison is on half allowance. My brother mentions the return of our 2nd Battalion to England, but they are now ordered to Jersey. At present there is no probability of me being ordered to join them. I returned the letters I received from Mr. Wood when at Lisbon, under cover of a letter I wrote you. Chadk. says Mr. James Orrel is anxious to hear from his brother. I mentioned in my last that he is in General Hill's army in the Alentigo. I am anxiously waiting an answer to my letter of the 8th Oct. I also wrote you on the 4th ult. No doubt you have received both by this time. Our officers and men continue sickly. In our last advance we left nine officers in the rear, but I am thankful my health continues good; better if possible than when in England. We have no news here that is interesting, but are all expecting to advance.

P.S.—My brother mentions that Startem has been to school to John Lee, but is a great blockhead. I therefore am sorry to hear that he is a favourite with my sister, but I trust he will provide another dog against my return, and send it to the same master. You must not forget to remember me to John Lee, and tell him there is plenty of game. One of his dogs would be invaluable if with the army. A spaniel which he would not harbour was yesterday sold for 100 dollars.

To his father Robert Knowles

Villa de Serva, Dec. 31st, 1811—The army is still in the same quarters, but we are daily expecting a move. It is supposed that Ciudad Rodrigo will be Lord Wellington's first object, as he is making preparations for a siege. Detachments from each regiment in the 4th Division are employed making gabions and fascines for the erection of batteries, and the battering-train have orders to be in readiness to march at an hour's notice. He has also thrown a bridge over the Aqueda about eight miles from this village and six from Ciudad Rodrigo. The French have detached two divisions of their army, and have evacuated Placentia. If we do advance I hope our regiment will be in the front, as I would prefer fighting to lying in the trenches at this season. The Spaniards annoy the French a great deal in this part of the country. General Mina alone destroyed seven thousand of them the last month. I have not heard from home since the 30th Sept., but suppose your letters must have miscarried. I did not neglect drinking your good health on Christmas Day, nor that of all my absent friends, but must say I envied their situation sitting by a fireside with their bellies full of Christmas pies, but if they are feasting upon all the luxuries England can afford I shall enjoy them the more when I return, with this satisfaction, that I have fought for my country abroad. While writing the above I received a pressing invitation from Captain King, of our regiment, to dine with him and Major Despard. The only news I can give you is that we shall break ground before Ciudad Rodrigo on the 13th inst., for you must know it is now the New Year, and I have the satisfaction to wish you every pleasure this world can afford. If I do not hear from you in answer to a letter of the 8th October in a few days, I shall be under the necessity of drawing a bill upon you for £20. The last letter I wrote you was of the 3rd ult., but have no doubt you have received it by this time. The army is not so sickly as it was when I last wrote, and it gives me great pleasure to say I remain in perfect health.

CHAPTER 3

1812

The New Year was heralded in for the Allied army by the capture of Ciudad Rodrigo, which Wellington had persistently blockaded.

The foregoing letter tells of making preparation for the siege in connection with which it gives even a date! The 1st, 3rd, 4th, and Light Divisions were selected for this duty, each division taking its turn in rotation. They had, to cross a river, wading sometimes up to the waist, to reach the trenches. The winter was unusually severe, and the Troops suffered great hardships. On January 8th, the Light Division, making a circuit, took up a position distant three miles from the fortress. In the evening that distinguished soldier, Colonel John Colborne, at the head of two Companies from each of the Regiments of the Light Division, carried by assault the palisaded redoubt Francisco, which was close to the "Greater Tesson," the farther of the two ridges on the north side. The operation was well managed by the stormers, whose loss was but trifling, and during the night they made a parallel of 600 yards.

On the 10th, the 4th Division were in the trenches, and opened communications from the parallel to the batteries. By the 19th, the breaches became practicable; and, as there was a probability that Marmont might attempt to relieve the fortress, Lord Wellington decided to carry it by assault. His final order showed the confidence which he had in his soldiers. It ended with the imperative command—"Ciudad Rodrigo must be stormed this evening". The storming was committed to the 3rd and Light Divisions, and the Portuguese under General Pack. The 4th Division was held in reserve.

The operation was divided into three attacks, right, centre, and left, with a false attack upon the St. Jago gate, at the opposite side of the town. The troops in the right attack were to cross the Águeda river, and escalade an outwork in front of the castle. Colonel O'Toole of the Cacadores was in command. The centre attack was to be made by the 3rd Division, Major Manners commanding the storming-party of five hundred Volunteers, and Major George Napier commanding three hundred men of the Light Division.

All were in their appointed places when the attack was prematurely commenced on the right. The storming parties rushed, with astonishing speed under a heavy fire, into the breaches. The main body of the 3rd Division were the first to get in, and for a short time they drove the French before them; but, they were held up by a tempest of grape and musket-fire, and by the filling-up of the passages with the bodies of the dead and wounded. The stormers of the Light Division jumped into the dark ditch, eleven feet deep, and soon found their way up to the smaller breach, which was so narrow that one gun was sufficient to block it. The officers dashed into it followed by their men, while the supports followed rapidly, and at this point the fortress was won.

The 43rd enfiladed the defenders, and the explosion of the magazines at the same time helped the 3rd Division to get in at the centre, the Portuguese on the right gaining also the positions assigned to them. For a short time there was some fighting in the streets; but, soon all was over, and the Governor, who was in the castle, surrendered his sword to Lieutenant Gurwood, the leader of the "forlorn hope" of the Light Division.

The French lost 300 killed and 1,500 wounded, while 150 guns with much ammunition were captured. The Allies lost 90 officers and 1,200 men killed and wounded; of these, 60 officers and 650 men were killed, or wounded, at the breaches. Among the slain were Generals Craufurd and Mackinnon.

The former was mortally wounded while directing the attack on the lesser breach, and died a few days afterwards. "A man of great ability" is his description by one who loved him not. He was a stern disciplinarian and a capable Commander, both liked and feared by the men of the Light Division, whom he had brought as fighting soldiers to the highest point of perfection. In seven minutes the Light Division was packed and under arms ready to march or take its place in a line of battle: and this, not on special occasions, but always. It is the leader-ship that tells, and the 43rd, 52nd, and 95th (now the Rifle Brigade) Regiments were indeed fortunate to have been trained by two Commanders of the eminence of Sir John Moore and General Robert Craufurd. The personality of Craufurd remained with the Light Division long after he had died. The mortal remains of that intrepid warrior were laid in the breach of the bastion that he had won, and it still bears his name. General Mackinnon was beloved by all who knew him, including Napoleon, with whom, strange to relate, he had been a friend in his youth.

Sir William Napier, who was present with his regiment, the 43rd, says:

> There died many gallant men, amongst others a Captain of the 45th, of whom it has been felicitously said, that three Generals and seventy other officers had fallen, but the soldiers, fresh from the strife, only talked of Hardyman.

Many more details are given in the two following letters.

TO HIS FATHER ROBERT KNOWLES

Castelheo, January 20th, 1812—It gives me great pleasure to inform you that Ciudad Rodrigo has surrendered to our arms. In my last I mentioned the probability of our besieging that fortress. On the 8th instant we marched from our cantonment to St. Felius Chico, near which place we crossed the river Aqueda. The same evening the Light Division took by storm a strong outwork within 400 yards of Ciudad Rodrigo, and broke ground about the same distance from the fortress. On the 9th, the 1st Division relieved the Light; on the 10th we relieved the 1st, and on the 11th the 3rd Division relieved us. The whole duties of the siege have been carried on by the four divisions I have mentioned. The works were carried on briskly under showers of shot from the enemy, and three battery's were completed, and the guns opened about three o'clock on the evening of the 14th instant. I was on duty in one of the battery's at the time, and consider myself a lucky fellow to escape without a scratch, as my party had the dangerous duty of opening the embrasures for the guns, and the enemy's fire was directed altogether at us. A very fine young man, a lieutenants in the Engineers, was mortally wounded when standing by my side. Our guns played their part well, and in one hour silenced all the enemy's guns in their front. Our guns continued to batter in breach until the 19th, when the breach was reported practicable, and the Light Division ordered to assist the division on duty to storm the place. Our division was relieved on the 19th by the Third, but the Fusilier Brigade was detained until three o'clock, and we fully expected to share with the Third and Light Divisions the honor of storming the town, and were much annoyed at being ordered into quarters at this village. It is the most painful part of my duty to state the loss it is supposed we have sustained in storming the town, which commenced about seven o'clock in the evening. The 45th and 88th Regiments. were the first to enter the breach, and, of course, have suffered the most. It is said we lost about 500 men, including about thirty-five officers. General Crawford is mortally wounded, Colonel Colborne, of the 52nd, killed. General Mackinnon, of the Guards, was killed by the blowing up of a magazine after the town had surrendered; but, you will see the particulars of the siege and the loss we have sustained in the *Gazette*. I believe our regiment, in the whole of the siege has not lost more than fifteen men. We fully expect to march tomorrow, whether to the front or return to our old quarters is uncertain. The garrison of Ciudad Rodrigo are marched as prisoners to Almeada today.

P. S.—I have not received a letter from home since the 30th Sept., and we have accounts from England up to the 31st Dec. You must be aware, as I mentioned in a former letter, that the postage of all letters from abroad must be paid in England, otherwise they will not be forwarded.

> The writer was here in error, as Colonel Colborne survived until 1863. Colonel Colborne was for many years known as Sir John Colborne, until he became Field-Marshal Lord Seaton. A distinguished soldier who, upon many occasions, proved himself to be capable of turning the fate of a battle.
>
> In a letter, dated one month later, there are given further details connected with the taking of Ciudad Rodrigo. There were twenty deserters found in the fortress: some were shot, some were otherwise punished, and some were forgiven:

To his father Robert Knowles

Almada, February 18th, 1812—After the lapse of several months I have the pleasure to acknowledge the receipt of a letter from my brother of so late a date as the 29th ult. I have wrote you since the fall of Ciudad Rodrigo, since which time there has nothing particular occurred. We marched a few days ago from castlejos through Ciudad Rodrigo to Carpió, and yesterday we came to this village, but I do not suppose we shall remain here many days, as it is believed the greatest part of the army will gradually move to the south, and then we expect to be amused by the siege of Badajos. We have had a hard day's work, the whole of our division having been assembled to see the sentence of a General Court Martial put in force on two deserters, who were taken in Ciudad Rodrigo. They were sentenced to be shot; it was the most awful sight I ever beheld. My brother asks if any of the Bolton lads are present. I only know one that is with the regiment., of the name of Robinson. I will make enquiries after the others, and write you in my next. He also asks after two men of the name of Jackson; if he will write me when they were enlisted, and where they come from, I will make enquiry after them. I was obliged to break off my letter here to perform the most melancholy part of my duty. I was called upon to superintend the funeral of a poor fellow in my company. It would astonish some of my acquaintances in England to see me acting in the place of a clergyman, reading the burial service, etc. Our regiment is still very sickly, and I am sorry to say the mortality is very great, numbers of our poor fellows dying after three or four days' sickness. I mentioned in some of my letters that I should be under the necessity of drawing a bill upon you for £20, but the kindness of a friend has rendered it unnecessary, but hope you will on receipt of this pay into the hands of Messrs. Greenwood and Co., army agents, the sum of £20 to be placed to the account of Lieutenant H. F. Devey, of our regiment, and desire the Agents to write him on the receipt of it. I beg you will not lose any time in lodging the money, and be particular in desiring them to write to him without loss of time, as it will be his only receipt for it. I shall anxiously wait an answer to this letter.

THE THIRD SIEGE OF BADAJOZ

The third attempt to capture Badajoz, a Spanish town and fortress on the Portuguese border, began on March 15th, 1812, when Marshal Beresford invested the fortress with the 3rd, 4th, and Light Divisions, and a Portuguese brigade, a force in all of 15,000 men. Badajoz was defended by 5,000 French, Hessian, and Spanish soldiers under a resolute, resourceful French officer, General Armand Phillipon, who had stored provisions both for the citizens and for the garrison, sufficient to last three months: but, he was short of ammunition.

The town stands where a small stream, the Rivillas, runs into the Guadiano, and the defences consisted of curtains and bastions, from 23 to 30 feet high, with counterscarps. There was a castle with numerous outworks, including San Roque, the Picurina, a redoubt 400 yards from the town, the Pardaleras, between the Guadiano and Rivillas and 200 yards from the ramparts, but connected therewith and defended by powerful batteries: these were all on the left bank of the Guadiano. On the right bank stood the fort of San Cristobal, which overlooked the interior of the castle, and on the western side of it was the redoubt of San Vincente, with three forts, which were mined. The arch of the bridge of San Roque was built up to make an inundation, 18 feet deep. These, briefly, were the main defences.

In the two sieges of 1811, the plan of operations was to assault the castle, at the south-eastern corner of the fortress, and the redoubt Cristobal. On this occasion, for various reasons, it was decided to attack the bastions of Trinidad and Santa Maria; but, before this could be attempted, the Picurina hill had to be stormed and captured. Preparatory for this, the first communication and parallel were made on March 17th, and, one week later, on March 25th, after stupendous difficulties caused by floods and other untoward circumstances, all was ready for the attack. The redoubt was stronger than its appearance indicated; but, in the night of the 25th, General Kempt with 500 men of the 3rd Division carried it by assault, when 319 officers and men were killed or wounded.

Time was running against Wellington. Marshal Soult with an army was approaching him. He sent, therefore, General Graham's Division to take up a position at Albuera to which he purposed withdrawing all but an investing force, and there to offer battle, should the necessity arise. But Wellington's soldiers were fiercely eager for the fray, and, the breaches being considered practicable, an order went forth that the fortress was to be stormed in the night of April 6th. General Picton's Division, "the fighting 3rd", was to cross the Rivillas stream, and escalade the castle wall, while Major Wilson of the 48th Regiment, with the Guards of the trenches, was to attack San Roque. This was the right attack. In the centre, the 4th and Light Divisions under General Colville and Colonel Barnard were to assault and force the breaches. To the 4th Division was assigned the Trinidad, and to the Light Division the bastion of Santa Maria. Each attack was preceded by forlorn hopes and storming parties of 500 men. The 5th Division while making a feint on Pardaleras were to carry the bastion of San Vincente.

On that dark evening there was but little to show the volcanic forces that lay hidden within the fortress. An occasional light, and the voices of the sentinels on the ramparts passing the report that all was well, gave no indication or hint to the besiegers that the garrison were alert and prepared with every means that the ingenuity of a capable and experienced Commander could devise for the destruction of their assailants. The British longed for the hour when they would be let loose at the fortress: they were galled by the prolonged restraint, and they hated sieges. The digging and excavating, the long hours in crouching attitudes in wet and muddy trenches, exhausted their patience and irritated them, until their temper was one of suppressed, frenzied, anger. Wellington's order was for a simultaneous attack at 10 o'clock, but a fire-ball or "carcase", to use the soldiers' term, thrown from the castle disclosed the position and readiness of the 3rd Division, and they were consequently obliged to make an attack, premature by half an hour. The 4th and Light Divisions were compelled to move at the same time, silently and quickly, to the breaches. Major Wilson's detachment consisted of the guards of the trenches, and with these were fifty men of the Royal Fusiliers under Lieutenant Knowles. This was the first party to effect the capture of any portion of the defence, and what happened is best told by Lieutenant Knowles in a letter to his father dated June 19th, 1812.

The 3rd Division crossed the Rivillas, but were met with a heavy stream of musketry fire. Rushing forward they placed the scaling ladders against the walls of the castle, and rapidly ascended, only to meet with a terrible fire. The ladders were pushed from the walls, heavy blocks of wood, crushing all beneath, were thrown upon them. They fell back to the shelter of the hill, where they were re-formed. Colonel Ridge of the 5th Fusiliers, in a loud voice called upon his men to follow him, and rushing forward placed a ladder against a lower part of the wall, near an embrasure: another officer, Ensign Canch, placed a second ladder close to the first: and, in a moment, both officers were on the ramparts, their men crowding after them. The French, astounded by such daring, were driven into the town, and the castle was won, but it was not to be retained if the enemy could prevent it. Bringing up their reserves, they attacked the castle at the main town entrance, but were repulsed, at the cost of the life of that gallant leader, Colonel Ridge, who was shot through the bars of the gate.

Glancing at that part of this terrible fight, where the Light and 4th Divisions were engaged, it is necessary to take the main incidents of the struggle of the two divisions in their proper sequence. The stormers of the Light Division, led by the heroic Major O'Hara, rushed forward, jumped into the ditch, and placed their ladders against the walls of the Santa Maria. A bright flashing light, coming as from the earth, illuminated the whole scene, and showed to the defenders who were crowded on the ramparts, the heavy swinging columns of the two British divisions, following their respective storming parties. Suddenly, there was a deafening explosion of shell, powder, and powder-barrels, which hurled the storming-parties to atoms. The Light Division were for a moment appalled by the spectacle; but, rending the air with a loud angry shout, they leaped into a ditch. At this moment, the 4th Division came running up, and poured in to the sunken fray. In one place the bottom of the ditch had been scooped out, and filled with water, and into this one hundred men fell and were drowned. They belonged to the two Fusilier Regiments, the 7th and 23rd—the men of Albuera. Those who followed turned to the left and came on the face of the unfinished ravelin. This was mistaken for the breach: but, between the ravelin and the ramparts there was a yawning chasm. Again baffled, there was great confusion as the two divisions crowded in the ravelin. They made an unexpected rush for the breach, but there across the top glittered a range of sword-blades, keen-edged on both sides, firmly fixed in heavy beams. It was impossible to gain a firm foot-hold, as loose planks studded with nails were laid in the narrow pathway, causing each man who tried to stand on them to fall. The attempt to force an entrance was made again and again. Colonel Macleod of the 43rd was shot in the breach. Two hours of this fruitless carnage convinced the officers and men that they could not get through the breach in the Trinidad, or the Santa Maria. The main attack had failed and 2,000 men had fallen in the effort.

About midnight, Lord Wellington ordered the two divisions to retire from the breaches, so as to prepare for a second assault. The 3rd Division still held the castle. General Walker's brigade of the 5th Division had escaladed the bastion of San Vincente and, fighting their way along the ramparts and into the town, had captured three bastions as they went. The fighting in the town continued for some time, then once more it turned to the ramparts, where its course was checked, and then it turned again back into the town. Finding that the British were momentarily increasing their numbers in the town, the French withdrew from the defence of the breaches, and Badajoz was won, and won, not by the troops of the main attack, but by the 3rd Division which forced its way into the castle—an inspiration of Sir Thomas Picton, who begged that he might be allowed to assault the castle—by Walker's brigade at San Vincente, and, in some degree, by the guards of the trenches under Wilson.

General Phillipon, who was wounded, surrendered on the following morning.

In this assault, no less than 3,500 British officers and men fell, and, of these, 60 officers and 700 men were killed on the spot. At the breaches the 4th and Light Division each lost 1,200 men, and of the 7th Fusiliers, 5 officers and 44 men were killed, and 13 officers and 121 men were wounded.

This letter, undated, but written on April 7th, 1812, the day after the capture of the town of Badajos, gives some vivid personal experiences:

To his father Robert Knowles

Camp before Badajos—It gives me great pleasure to be able to write you after the bloody business on the night of the 6th. At the commencement of the business I had the honourable command of a party of 40 men of our regiment, which, with others of the division, to the number of 150, under the command of Captain Horton, of the 23rd, were ordered to storm the ravelin, a strong outwork about 100 yards from the town, defended on one side by water and a wall around it about 24 feet in height. After being exposed for half an hour to the hottest fire I was ever under, we succeeded in placing one ladder against the wall, by which my party entered. A corporal was the first who got into the fort, and was immediately killed. I was the third man who mounted the ladder. On leaping into the place I was knocked down by a shower of grape which broke my sabre into a hundred pieces. I providentially escaped without any serious injury, although my clothes were torn from my back. My sword hand is much cut and bruised, which accounts for my bad writing, and my right side is a little bruised. As I mentioned to you before, my sword was broken in pieces. I therefore picked up my corporal's firelock, and with the assistance of eight or ten men who had now got into the fort, I charged along the ramparts, destroying or disarming all who opposed us. The French garrison consisted of 150 men, but we only took and destroyed about 60, the remainder made their escape to the town. We found 5 guns in the fort. After properly securing the fort, we advanced to assist in the attack of the town. You will see the particulars of the whole business in the *Gazette*, and as my hand is very painful I must conclude. Suffice it to say our regiment, is cut to pieces; we lost 5 officers killed and 12 wounded; our wounded officers will leave the camp this morning, when there will be only ten officers with the regiment, and scarcely one of them without a bruise. The post will leave the camp at 10 o'clock, but I will write you by the next.

P.S.—Lieutenant Wray, whom my brother has often mentioned, is one of the unfortunate officers who fell in the breach of Badajos.

Sir William Napier concludes the narrative of this assault with a splendid testimony:

> Let any man picture to himself this frightful carnage taking place in a space of less than one hundred square yards. Let him consider that the slain died not all suddenly, nor by one manner of death; that some perished by steel, some by shot, some by water, that some were crushed and mangled by heavy weights, some trampled upon, some dashed to pieces by the fiery explosions; that for hours this destruction was endured without shrinking, and that the town was won at last;—Let any man consider this and he must admit that a British army bears with it an aw-

ful power. Who shall do justice to the bravery of the soldiers? the noble emulation of the officers? who shall measure out the glory of Ridge, of Macleod, of Nicholas, or of O'Hara of the 95th, who perished on the breach at the head of the stormers, and with him nearly all the volunteers of that desperate service. No action, no age ever sent forth braver troops to battle than those who stormed Badajoz.

O'Hara, when leaving camp for the assault, remarked, "a lieutenant-colonel, or dead-meat, to-morrow."

THE BATTLE OF SALAMANCA

The fortress of Ciudad Rodrigo fell in January, and Badajoz in April, and yet the campaign of this year did not begin until June when both armies were assembled for a mighty contest in the open field.

The Royal Fusiliers, with the 4th Division, crossed the Tagus on April 20th, and were quartered at Valongas. The movements of the regiment and indeed of the army, is well described in the letter from Salamanca of June 19th, 1812, which is a connecting link in the events between the fall of Badajoz, and the movements leading up to the defeat of the French at Salamanca. It gives, moreover, a precise narrative of the part taken by the detachment under the command of Lieutenant Knowles in the storming and capture of San Roque:

TO HIS FATHER ROBERT KNOWLES

Camp near Salamanca, June 19th, 1812—I wrote you last on the 7th April, the day after the storming of Badajos, and promised to write you again by the next post, but the nature of the wound in my hand rendered it impossible, although it did not prevent me marching with my regiment, to the north of Portugal. On our arrival at Valango I was attacked with a slow fever, from which I barely recovered when we marched from those quarters on the 5th instant. I was sent to Celonio, in charge of the sick of the division, but on my arrival obtained leave to rejoin my regiment, and by making a few days forced marches I joined them in camp near Ciudad Rodrigo on the 12th inst. On the 13th, 14th, 15th, and 16th we marched toward Salamanca. On the night of the 16th the enemy evacuated the town, but have left a garrison in two convents which .they have fortified. Our battery are in a forward state, and it is expected will open upon their works to-morrow morning. The 6th Division and two German regiments are quartered in the town, and carry on the dutys of the siege. The Light Division and 3rd Division are in the front of us, about two miles. Ours and the 5th Division are encamped on the banks of the Tormes, a most beautiful river which runs close by the town of Salamanca. The 1st and 7th Divisions are on our right; they are also encamped on the banks of the river. I yesterday went over to see the town. The cathedral surpasses in grandeur anything I ever saw, and the town excels in every respect any that I have seen in this country. As soon as we have taken the enemy's works at Salamanca, it is supposed we shall advance with the greatest rapidity into the heart of Spain, as it is supposed Marmont cannot collect an army strong enough to fight us. I mentioned to you in my last that I was not with my regiment, at the storming of Badajos, but on duty in the trenches. Major Wilson, 48th Regiment, received orders to attack with 300 men Fort St. Roque (or the ravelin). Our regiment, furnished 50 men for that duty. I applied and succeeded in obtaining the command of them. When the 3rd Division commenced their attack upon the castle we advanced to the ravelin, and after considerable difficulty we succeeded in placing one ladder against the wall, about 24 feet high. A corporal of mine was the first to mount it, and he was killed at the top of it. I was the third or fourth, and when in the act of leaping off the wall into the fort I was knocked down by a discharge from the enemy, the handle of my sabre broke into a hundred pieces, my hand disabled, and at the same time I received a very severe bruise on my side, and a slight wound, a piece of lead (having penetrated through my haversack, which was nearly filled with bread, meat, and a small stone brandy-bottle for the use of the trenches during the night) lodged upon one side of my ribs, but without doing me any serious injury. I recovered myself as soon as possible, and by the time seven or eight of my brave fellows had got into the fort, I huzzaed and charged along the ramparts, killing or destroying all who opposed us. I armed myself with the first Frenchman's firelock I met with, and carried it as well as I was able under my arm. The greater part of my party having joined me, we charged into the body of the fort, when they all cried out "Prisoners." I forgot to mention to you the plan of attack: 150 men were to escalade on each side, but by some mistake they all attacked on the contrary side to what I did, and I have the satisfaction to state that my party let them all in at the gates. All the British troops from the trenches were ordered to support the 3rd Division in the castle, and Major Wilson gave me charge of the fort, with the remains of my party. From the end of a wall where I seated myself, I had a fine view of the different attacks upon the town. We secured about 60 prisoners, who had concealed themselves in different parts of the fort, and we killed and wounded about twenty-five. My party suffered severely. My sergeant and corporal were killed, and about twenty-five men killed and wounded.[1]

> The forts at Salamanca were captured on June 27th. Seven hundred prisoners, thirty guns, provisions, and a secure passage over the Tormes, were the reward of this success, which was achieved ten days earlier than Marshal Marmont thought possible. Fearing to give his opponent any advantage from a chosen position, Marmont retired, followed by Wellington. On July 18th, the 4th and Light

1. The remainder of this letter is missing.

Divisions with a brigade of cavalry were engaged all day with several French columns, and the 7th Fusiliers had twenty men wounded. There now occurred one of those instances of strange friendliness between contending armies which were not infrequent in the Peninsular Campaign. The British divisions were marching in column, the Light Division being nearest the French, but separated from them by the German cavalry. Both armies were moving at a rapid pace for the Guarena river, and the officers on each side, pointing their swords or waving their hands in courtesy, alternated their salutations with loud commands, while they passed from front to rear of their men, to quicken the pace towards the common goal. Such were the civilities between the officers of both armies.

On the morning of July 22nd, Marshal Marmont brought more troops within the zone of fire, and occupied a wooded height on which stood an old chapel. Close by were two hills called the Arapiles, by which name the battle of Salamanca is known to the Spaniards to this day. Wellington seized the farther of the two, while the French occupied the second, and at the same time he sent some companies of the Guards and Royal Fusiliers to drive the enemy out of the village of Arapiles. Wellington, who himself witnessed this action, was so pleased with the manner in which the Fusiliers did their work that he mentioned the name of Captain Crowder in his despatch. The 4th Division was in position on a ridge behind the village, while the 5th and 6th were drawn into the inner slopes of the Arapiles. The 3rd Division under General Pakenham was in a wood near Aides Tejada, where they were hidden from the enemy, while they commanded the main road to Ciudad Rodrigo. The interval between the 3rd and 4th Divisions was occupied by Bradford's Portuguese brigade, the Spaniards, and the British cavalry.

Wellington's position was now a strong one, and his hope was that Marmont would attack him. At 2 p.m., when at dinner, he received word that the French were moving towards the road to Ciudad Rodrigo. At once, he mounted his horse and earnestly watched the moving columns of the enemy. At 3 p.m., when their left was entirely separated from the centre, he said, "Marmont's good genius has forsaken him," and he issued the orders that brought on the battle.

The 5th Division formed on the right of the 4th Division, and, with the Portuguese and cavalry, presented a front to the enemy. The 6th and 7th Divisions, British cavalry and Spaniards, prolonged the line in the direction of the 3rd Division. When these dispositions were completed, Wellington ordered the 3rd Division, with 12 guns and a brigade of cavalry to cross the enemy's line of march. To his brother-in-law, General Pakenham, the Commander of the 3rd Division in Picton's absence, he said, pointing to the column of Thomières, "Ned, do you see those fellows? Throw your division into column and drive them to the devil."

The reply was, "Yes: but, let me grasp that conquering right hand".

As Pakenham's attack developed, the remainder of the first line was ordered to attack. When Marmont saw the 3rd Division break across the path of his column on the Ciudad Rodrigo road, he was dismayed. At 5 o'clock, Pakenham began the battle by falling on the front of the French column as it emerged from a wood, while his guns took it in flank. Disconnected, and with many men still in the wood, it was taken at a great disadvantage, and Pakenham pushed home his success with terrible force. The 4th Division, under General Lowry Cole, deployed into line and, with the 5th, passing the Arapiles village and crossing some heavy ploughed land under a storm of grape, drove General Bonnet's troops back, step by step, to the southern and eastern height. The Royal Fusiliers under Major Beatty, in the front line, carried a height and captured 18 guns.

The failure of the Portuguese to secure the second of

the two Arapiles, left the 7th Fusiliers at the mercy of the French cavalry and infantry. Lieutenant Cameron who was present thus describes their position:

> We were at this moment ordered by Major Beatty to retire and form square, a most hazardous movement when the enemy's infantry were advancing, and within thirty yards of us. The order was only partially heard and obeyed on the right, while on the left we kept up a hot fire on the enemy, who were advancing up-hill, and within a few yards of us. The companies on our right having retired in succession, we found ourselves alone; but, the ground the enemy was ascending was so steep, that we got off without loss. Luckily, while we were forming square to receive cavalry, the 6th Division came up and received the charge intended for us.

Marmont and General Bonnet were wounded, Thomières was killed, and though General Bertrand Clausel with wonderful ability restored the battle, the repulse in the first forty minutes, after 5 o'clock, was never really recovered. The fight, however, continued until 10 o'clock, when, under cover of the darkness, Clausel skilfully withdrew, and, from the disordered masses, formed a rear-guard and covered the retreat. The allies lost over 7,000 in killed and wounded; but, the French loss was not less than 12,000, and 7,000 prisoners and eleven guns. The Royal Fusiliers lost one officer and 19 men killed, 10 officers and 170 men wounded.

Thus ended what is considered Wellington's most brilliant battle. The lightning-like stroke when Marmont separated his left from the centre, the screening from the enemy of his own dispositions, his holding back the reserves until the supreme moment, when their appearance seemed to the French to be that of an army suddenly arising from the ground, are indisputable proofs of good generalship.

This brief outline will help to explain the following letter of Lieutenant Knowles, written three days after the battle, when he was still suffering from the wound in his arm.

To his father Robert Knowles

Salamanca, July 25th, 1812—It is with the greatest satisfaction I write you after the glorious victory of the 22nd instant on the heights of Salamanca. The action commenced about four o'clock, by the enemy driving in our light infantry, when our regiment, was ordered to their support, and we drove them back in great style. Immediately a general attack commenced. Our brigade and a brigade of Portuguese advanced in line against their centre, the enemy keeping an incessant fire upon us from twelve pieces of artillery, but nothing could check our advance, and the enemy retired from the heights they occupied in the greatest confusion. At the same time General Packenham, with the 3rd Division, attacked and turned their left, taking a great number of prisoners, and several pieces of artillery. The enemy again formed upon some heights in front of a large forest, and we commenced a second attack. The enemy, after an obstinate resistance, ran into the woods, great numbers of them throwing away their arms. At the same time the 1st Division turned their right, when the rout became general. Our loss on this memorable day has been very severe:—Generals Le Marchant and Pack killed, Generals Beresford, Cotton, Leith, Cole, Clinton, and many other officers of rank wounded. The enemy's loss is estimated at from 10 to 12 thousand men killed and wounded, and upwards of four thousand prisoners, with a great number of guns, eagles, and colours. Early in the morning our army commenced its pursuit, and they have already sent through this town upwards of 4,000 more prisoners. You may calculate upon the destruction of one-half the French army, as our army is in full pursuit about 40 miles from this town on the road to Madrid. The French Commissariat have all ran away; they have no bread or meat, and are killing their horses as a substitute. At the conclusion of the action I received a musket ball in my left arm, but I had it cut out the same night, and I believe the bone is not injured.

Our regiment, as usual, has suffered considerably, one captain killed, one captain wounded, and nine lieutenants Our brigade does not exceed 500 men, and they are formed into one battalion. Our loss fell chiefly upon the 3rd, 4th, 5th, and 6th Divisions. The 1st, 7th, and Light Divisions are in high order, and with the cavalry are strong enough to fight the enemy if they dare to make a stand. I wrote you last from camp near this town about the 18th ult. We remained in the neighbourhood covering the operations against the fort at this town. The enemy lay in our front, and sometimes amused us with a brisk cannonade. The 7th Division had a sharp skirmish, driving the enemy from a hill on our right. On the 26th the enemy retired, and the fort having surrendered, we pursued them. On the 27th the enemy retired upon Toursde Selas,[2] where they crossed the Douro. We remained in camp on the opposite side the river near Medina del Campo, until the night of the 15th. On the morning of the 18th the enemy came up with us. A heavy cannonade commenced which lasted the whole day. In the evening they came up with us, and their infantry attempted to turn our left, but were repulsed with great slaughter by the left brigade of our division, supported by the Portuguese. Another French column advanced, and we advanced to meet them, but they thought proper to retire in double quick time. On the 20th we again retired. On the 21st we had a great deal of manoeuvring. On the morning of the 22nd there was a sharp skirmish, which lasted about four hours. Lord Wellington did all in his power to entice them upon a hill immediately in our front, which he at last succeeded in doing,

2. Read "Tordesillas." Marmont took the direction of the Douro and moved to Tordesillas—Gleig's Life of Wellington, p. 167.

and immediately a general attack commenced. Never did a British army carry on a campaign with so much success, the surprising General Gerard's Corps in the south, the capture of Ciudad Rodrigo, Badajos, then at Almarez, and Salamanca, lastly the destruction of one half the French army has placed our gallant leader amongst the greatest Generals[3] of modern Europe, and no recompense his country can make him will be too great. I will write you again by the next post, and give you all the news in my power.

P.S.—Excuse all mistakes and bad writing, as my arm is rather painful, and the post is going.

> The Royal Fusiliers accompanied Wellington to Madrid and took part in his triumphal entry into the Capital of Spain. It might have been a ceremonial exchange between Governors. At 6 o'clock in the morning of the 12th August, King Joseph with his court left, and at noon Wellington with his army marched into Madrid.
> Lieutenant Knowles made light of his wound in his home-letters; but, it was officially described as "severe", and, as he was suffering in addition from fever and ague, he was remaining at Salamanca. The evidence of this is circumstantially precise. It is, moreover, certain that his next letter, bearing the post mark "Lisbon, September 23rd, 1812," was written at Salamanca.

To his father Robert Knowles

I have been under the necessity of breaking my promise in my letter of the 25th ult., which was to write to you by the next post. I hope you have received it long before this, as it would satisfy you that my wound was of a trifling nature, and I am happy to say that it is now completely healed. Immediately

---

3. In *The Bible in Spain*, by George Borrow, the Spanish curé says that Wellington and General Craufurd dined in his house after the battle. Wellington may have dined there, but Craufurd was lying on the ramparts of Ciudad Rodrigo.

after closing my last letter to you, I was attacked by the ague fever and a most severe bowel complaint, with which I have ever since been confined to my bed, with the exception of four or five days. I trust that I have now banished all my complaints, as I have not had a fit of the ague this last three days, and I am rapidly recovering my strength. I yesterday rode as far as the field of battle, but found myself so very weak that I could not ride over the ground. Our wounded in this town are rapidly recovering, but the officers are extremely ill off, not having a farthing to purchase the comforts which are necessary to men nearly reduced to skeletons by wounds and sickness.

The army is only paid up to the 24th March, but they had the generosity to give to each wounded officer 20 dollars a few days after our arrival in this town. This sum (to a few who nursed it well) has supplied the necessaries of life; others have sold their horses, asses, or mules; others their epaulettes, watches, rings, etc., and, to the disgrace of John Bull, others have perished for want. These are the sufferings which British wounded officers have been subject to in this town, but thanks to Providence I have not been subject to the least inconvenience. Fortunately I had a few dollars in my possession when I came into the town, which have enabled me to get nearly all a person in my sickly situation could desire. You cannot expect news from me now that I am so far in the rear. The last accounts from the army they were still in quarters; the 1st, 4th, 5th, and 7th Divns. at the Esburial, the 3rd and Light Divns. at Madrid, the 6th Divn., with the 4th, 5th, 38th, 42nd, and 82nd Regiments were watching the remains of Marmont's army. Report says that General Maitland has landed at Alicante with an expedition from Sicily. We are anxious to hear what the Russians are doing. I hope they will keep the enemy employed in the north until this country is cleared of them. The Spaniards seem to be actively employed recruiting. The general outcry amongst them is "Let us have British officers and we will fight like British soldiers".

It is now about thirteen months since I left England, and I have in that time only received three letters from home, the last dated 29th February. It is natural to conclude that they could not always miscarry, and therefore that no one writes to me. The subject of Lieutenant Devey, which I have often wrote about, has given me a great deal of uneasiness. Whether you have lodged the £20 I have so repeatedly mentioned in his hands I am ignorant of. He is now returned to England on account of a wound and bad health. The last communication I had with him he proposed that I should give him your address, and he would write to you for the sum of ten pounds which I have received from him. On his arrival in England, therefore, if you have not lodged the money, I beg you will remit him the sum of ten pounds the first intimation you receive from him, and I also beg that you will pay the postage of all letters to him.

I have before stated to you that the army was six months in arrears of pay, which must be sufficient to show you at once my situation. I have lately been under the necessity of purchasing clothing, etc., to a considerable amount. I am therefore under the most disagreeable but pressing necessity of begging a further remittance of £25, which I request you will lodge in my name in the hands of Messrs. Greenwood and Co., army agents, and desire them to write to me on the receipt of it. By the same post you lodge the money I hope you will write me an account of it. It is extremely painful for me to ask this last remittance; nothing but real want should oblige me to do it.

I hope my health will shortly be re-established (it has been very precarious since the siege of Badajos). If it is not, I shall be under the necessity of effecting an exchange into a regiment serving in some other climate.

P.S.—As I do not receive letters from home, it may probably be owing to this circumstance that the postage of all letters for abroad must be paid in England, otherwise they will not be sent.

The condition of the wounded who were left at Salamanca was deplorable, and it remains a disgraceful reproach to the British Government of the day. They were without the actual necessities of life, many of them were in want of food, clothing, and medicines. The army was in arrears of pay, and the Commander-in-Chief had not the means for paying the butcher's bill. Many more of the sick and wounded would have died, but for the Commissary-General, Sir James McGrigor, who sent stores from Madrid on his own responsibility, without authority, and he was censured for so doing.

It is obvious that Lieutenant Knowles, on account of his wound and disease, was unequal for some months to march with his regiment, and to endure the hardships of the campaign. This explains his presence at the depot which was established at Santarem on the Tagus, about fifty miles from Lisbon.

There is now a gap in the correspondence; for, there is no letter between September 23rd, 1812 and February 7th, 1813, the last of the series, and this is much to be regretted. We can, however, imagine the spectacle of a high-spirited young officer, rejoicing in restoration to health, and chafing at the inaction of an enforced detention at a depot, when his regiment is in the field. A staff-appointment, with its daily increase of five shillings to a subaltern's pay, does not lessen his zeal to be with his comrades in the fighting-line, and, in June, he is again with his regiment.

CHAPTER 4

1813

To his father Robert Knowles

Santarem, February. 7th, 1813—I wrote you last from Lisbon on the 19th Dec, and returned to this on the 24th same month. I was so far recovered that I immediately applied for permission to join my regiment, but was unfortunately detained to do duty in this depot.

About three weeks ago I was ordered to act as Adjutant, and I am still pestered with that troublesome office. From nine o'clock in the morning till six in the evening I have not a spare minute. The constant employment I have had, and the uncertainty of remaining here, has been the cause of my delaying writing to you much longer than I intended. With my new office, I have become a man of business; every post-day I have eight or more letters to answer, and weekly we send in about fifty returns to headquarters. The commandant, in direct opposition to my wishes, has reported me to the Adjutant General as a stationary officer at this depot, so that I can see no prospect of leaving for some time.

The last letter I received from home was dated the 17th Nov. The late severe family losses you have sustained distress me excessively, but the miseries I have witnessed and partially endured in this country have in some measure hardened my feelings. It is a subject I cannot dwell upon, therefore will close it.

The last mail brought us the most glorious news from Russia; it appears to be almost incredible the success they have obtained over the common enemy. I now feel confident that the business in this country will be decided the ensuing summer, and that I shall soon have the satisfaction of returning to my native land, and conversing about my adventures in the Peninsula. We have no news at this depot, therefore must conclude.

P. S. *February 9th, 1813*—Our Lieutenant-Colonel Blakeney passed through this town this morning on his march to the army. I mentioned my being detained here, and my having been applied to for to accept the adjutancy of this depot. He strongly recommended me to join my regiment, but finding that I should not be allowed to do so at present, he advised me to accept the situation of adjutant., saying that, if I must be absent from my regiment, he saw no reason that I should not receive 5s. per day extra, so long as I should be detained. Until I write you the contrary, be so kind as to direct to me at Santarem.

In February, 1813, the Royal Fusiliers were at Castle Melhor, on the right bank of the Coa, and, towards the end of May, they crossed the Douro and marched to Salamanca. There is no record of the date when Lieutenant Knowles was released from the duties of Adjutant of the depot, or when he rejoined his regiment; but, it was most probably during May. From May 25th to June 19th, Wellington pursued the French, whose rearguard he caught on the left bank of the Bayas. With the Light Division he turned the enemy's left flank, attacking them at the same time in front with the 4th Division. The Fusilier Brigade now consisted of the 7th and 23rd Fusiliers, and the 20th and 48th regiments, under Major-General Robert Ross. They all participated in the attack made by the 4th Division. The 7th surprised the French in the village of Montevite, and, with the 20th, followed in pursuit, driving them across the river Zadora.

The Fusilier Brigade on the following day held a position on the banks of the Bayas, while the army was concentrating for a general attack. King Joseph Bonaparte had taken up a position six miles in length and in front of Vittoria, which stands on some rising ground. Wellington's plan of battle was to assail both flanks and, when they had been turned, to send three divisions against their front. The flank attacks were successful, and the frontal attack was set in motion, when with impetuosity the 3rd Division under Picton broke right through the French centre. With his centre broken and both flanks crushed in, King Joseph had no alternative but to retreat.

The last stand was made on some low hills where the fire of eighty guns checked Picton's victorious advance: but, the 4th Division rushing onwards stormed one hill and forced the French to retire from the others. The Royal Fusiliers took up a position at the bridge of Nanclares. The retreat of the French now became a running-fight for six miles, and, in the confusion and haste, they abandoned guns, baggage, and treasure to the value of one million sterling.

There were in some divisions of the army excesses; but, in spite of the temptation of rich spoils of war, the discipline of the Royal Fusiliers was such that they marched on, not a man leaving the ranks. On short rations for six weeks, and without food on the 21st, the day of the battle, the men were half starving, and, when they halted at 9 o'clock, they feasted with unbridled indulgence on the sheep, wine and biscuits, which the French had left behind them. The pursuit of the enemy was continued on the 22nd. After a long march, the 7th encamped in the neighbourhood of Pampeluna.

On July 18th, the 4th Division marched to the Pyrenees and took up a position in the valley of Urroz, the 7th being two miles in advance at Espinal. On the 24th, they were posted on a mountain to the west of Roncesvalles, in order to secure the pass. Marshal Soult, by whom King

Joseph Bonaparte had been superseded, finding the allies were holding a long scattered line, boldly determined to drive them from the Pyrenees. On the morning of July 25th, he fiercely attacked General Byng's brigade of the 2nd Division at Roncesvalles. While this combat was proceeding, the Fusilier Brigade advanced under General Ross, up the Mandechari pass, and at Lindouz they came suddenly upon the head of General Reille's column, which was pushing forward to secure the pass of Atalosti, and thus to cut off Campbell's Portuguese brigade.

Ross could act only on a very narrow front, yet he sent his foremost companies against the French column. This vigorous action secured the pass, and gave General Cole time to concentrate his forces: but, the pass was secured with the loss of many brave soldiers and, among them, was Lieutenant Robert Knowles, the only officer of the 7th Fusiliers who fell on that day.

Thus ended, in his twenty-fourth year, the career of this young Englishman. The space of his active military life was two years, but within that short period he had taken part in the two sieges of Ciudad Rodrigo and Badajoz, the action at Aldea da Ponte, and the battles of Salamanca and Vittoria. He suffered bodily-sickness from privations and hardships, and he was wounded twice. At Roncesvalles, he won a soldier's death.

There are two qualities which especially appear in the letters, namely, family affection and the bravery of the soldier. In Japan he would be an ancestor whose spirit would be the object of worship. His life was a fulfilment of the family motto: *nec diu nec frustta*—not for long, and not in vain.

His contemporaries, friends, and neighbours, showed their appreciation of his character and services by erecting to his memory a monument in the Parish Church of St. Peter, Bolton-le-Moors, Lancashire, which bears the following inscription:

To the memory of
Lieutenant Robert Knowles,
a native of this parish, who volunteered May 6th, 1811,
from the 1st Royal Lancashire Militia into the
7th Regiment of Fusiliers, then united with the British
army in the expulsion of the French from Spain.
He distinguished himself at the taking of Ciudad Rodrigo and at Badajos, where he commanded part of a
detachment appointed to storm Fort St. Roque.
Such was his intrepidity, that having first mounted the
wall and succeeded in his enterprise, he opened the gates
to the remainder of the detachment and received the
command of the fort. He behaved with much courage at
Salamanca and Vittoria, at the former of which places he
was severely wounded.
This brave young man fell in the hard-contested action
at the pass of Roncesvalles, in the Pyrenees, July 25th,
1813, in the 24th year of his age.

This monument is erected as a just tribute to so much
heroism and worth by his fellow townsmen, A.D. 1816.

LEONAUR

ALSO FROM LEONAUR

AVAILABLE IN SOFTCOVER OR HARDCOVER WITH DUST JACKET

CAPTAIN OF THE 95th (Rifles) *by Jonathan Leach*—An officer of Wellington's Sharpshooters during the Peninsular, South of France and Waterloo Campaigns of the Napoleonic Wars.

BUGLER AND OFFICER OF THE RIFLES *by William Green & Harry Smith* With the 95th (Rifles) during the Peninsular & Waterloo Campaigns of the Napoleonic Wars

BAYONETS, BUGLES AND BONNETS by *James 'Thomas' Todd*—Experiences of hard soldiering with the 71st Foot - the Highland Light Infantry - through many battles of the Napoleonic wars including the Peninsular & Waterloo Campaigns

THE ADVENTURES OF A LIGHT DRAGOON *by George Farmer & G.R. Gleig*—A cavalryman during the Peninsular & Waterloo Campaigns, in captivity & at the siege of Bhurtpore, India

THE COMPLEAT RIFLEMAN HARRIS *by Benjamin Harris as told to & transcribed by Captain Henry Curling*—The adventures of a soldier of the 95th (Rifles) during the Peninsular Campaign of the Napoleonic Wars

WITH WELLINGTON'S LIGHT CAVALRY *by William Tomkinson*—The Experiences of an officer of the 16th Light Dragoons in the Peninsular and Waterloo campaigns of the Napoleonic Wars.

SURTEES OF THE RIFLES by *William Surtees*—A Soldier of the 95th (Rifles) in the Peninsular campaign of the Napoleonic Wars.

ENSIGN BELL IN THE PENINSULAR WAR *by George Bell*—The Experiences of a young British Soldier of the 34th Regiment 'The Cumberland Gentlemen' in the Napoleonic wars.

WITH THE LIGHT DIVISION by *John H. Cooke*—The Experiences of an Officer of the 43rd Light Infantry in the Peninsula and South of France During the Napoleonic Wars

NAPOLEON'S IMPERIAL GUARD: FROM MARENGO TO WATERLOO by *J. T. Headley*—This is the story of Napoleon's Imperial Guard from the bearskin caps of the grenadiers to the flamboyance of their mounted chasseurs, their principal characters and the men who commanded them.

BATTLES & SIEGES OF THE PENINSULAR WAR by *W. H. Fitchett*—Corunna, Busaco, Albuera, Ciudad Rodrigo, Badajos, Salamanca, San Sebastian & Others